Colour and Design

for

Embroidery

Richard Box

Color and Design
for
Embroidery

A practical handbook for the daring embroiderer
and adventurous textile artist

Brassey's, Inc. • Washington, D.C.

Dedication

For Katherine

Acknowledgements

I am indebted to many individuals for their part in the production of this book. I now take this happy opportunity to give them my thanks for all their encouragement and help.

To Daphne Ashby, Irene Barnes, Jan Beaney, Ann Davies, Amanda Ewing, Rosalind Floyd, Robin Giddings, Margaret Hall-Townley, Elizabeth Hoare, Alison Holt, Paddy Killer, Maureen King , Jean Littlejohn, Andrew Lund, Pat McCoy, Rosemary Tindall and Verina Warren for allowing me to use their work or examples from their collections.

To the Royal School of Needlework and its principal, Elizabeth Elvin, for permission to use both historical and contemporary examples from its collection. The school's primary function is the training of young people to ensure that high standards in design and embroidery are maintained.

To the Editors: Venetia Penfold at the start and Simon Rosenheim at the end who did all the work.

To Michael Wicks for his beautiful photography.

To Pauline Garnham for her time and patience in typing the manuscript and putting it on file with her new computer.

First published in 2000 by
Brassey's, Inc.
22841 Quicksilver Drive
Dulles, VA 20166

Text and illustrations © Richard Box 2000
The moral right of the author has been asserted.

ISBN 1 57488 272 4

Printed in Spain

Photography by Michael Wicks unless otherwise stated

Contents

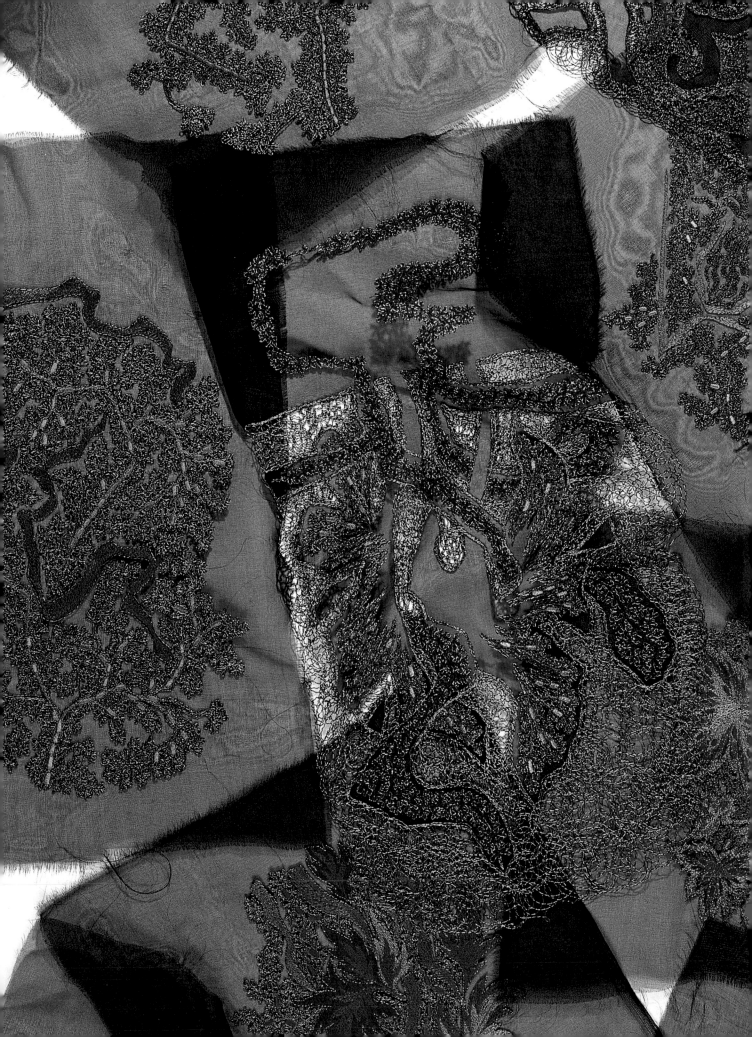

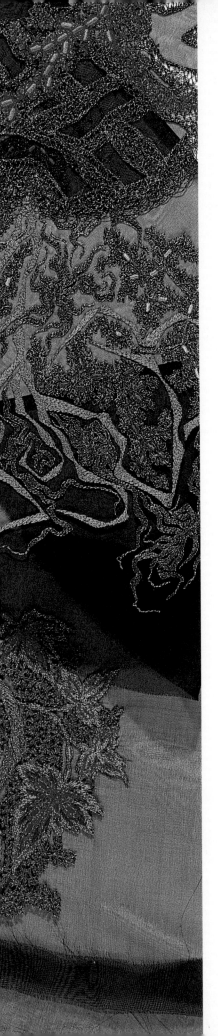

Preface

'The most important element in successful work is the choice of design, and I shall therefore be obliged to linger a little over this subject, as it is impossible to make a clear explanation to those of my readers to whom the subject may be entirely strange without a good deal of enlargement of general axioms. While inferior work can be tolerated for the sake of design, if that is good (though the two rarely go together), excellent work on a worthless design must be cast aside as labour lost; so that, you see, design is the very soul and essence of beautiful embroidery, as it is of every other art, exalted or humble. It is enough to break one's heart to see the labour and skill sometimes spent over a would-be decorative ornament, that instead of being full of beauty and intention, is more like a heterogeneous collection of unmeaning shapes, lacking form, which the designer himself, if put to it, could as ill explain as anyone else.'

May Morris
from *Decorative Needlework*
1893

PART ONE

INTRODUCTION

'It is not because things are
difficult that we do not dare;
it is because we do not dare
that they are difficult.'

Seneca

Do you dare to design? Or are you daunted by a feeling of
dread because you think it is going to be difficult? Be
encouraged by Seneca's statement; you have already dared to
read so far into this book, so why not read on? Experienced
professionals, serious amateurs and eager noviciates have
generously contributed to this book, who along with me
earnestly desire to inspire, motivate and encourage you to
design. Who knows? Your exclamation, '*I feel happier with a
needle in my hand*' may become, '*I now feel happy with a pencil
in my hand too*'. You may even discover that the concepts of
design which you dreaded and the process of designing which
daunted you will now become delightful.

   The purpose of this book is to provide both practical and
theoretical assistance to all of you who wish to understand
more about the principles of design which govern your
particular discipline in embroidery or in any of the textile arts.
It is illustrated with many kinds of embroidery but also with
some examples of other ways of using fabrics and threads in

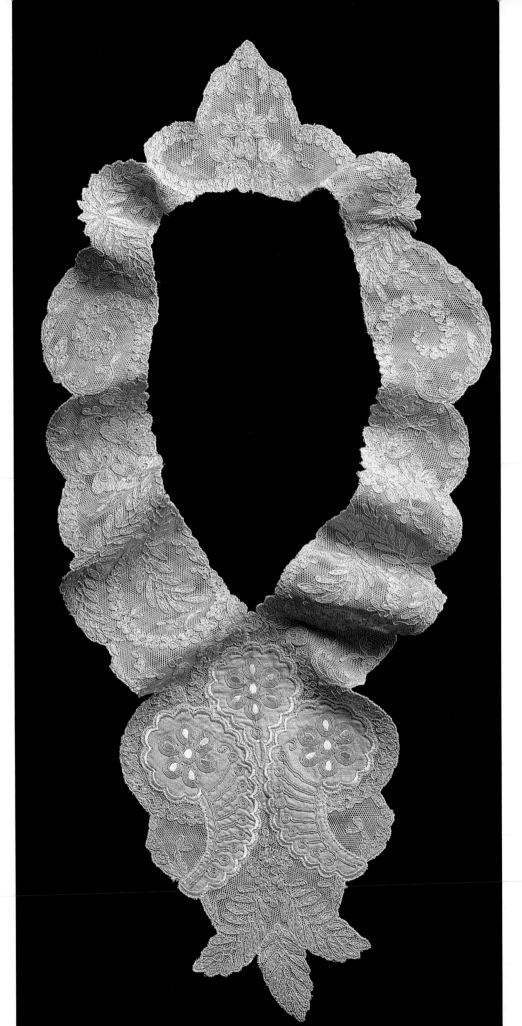

▸ Fig 2 Collar for
lingerie c1930. Schiffli
machine-embroidered
pieces on cotton lawn
with satin stitch
cording separately
sewn together on
two layers of net.
Private collection.

◂◂ Fig 1
Hand-embroidered
pin cushion by
Maureen King 1990s.

order to demonstrate the creative link between all textiles.

As you proceed through this book you will discover how the principles of design actually govern all forms of art and craft. No doubt many of you are already practising in a number of these disciplines and, indeed, even integrating them to create new forms. Many of you already know that once upon a time there was no artificial polarisation between those practising in the various disciplines of different forms of art and craft. Their hearts were united in the same creative process while producing individually distinctive forms. There have been periods during this last millennium when hierarchies have been formed and separatism rather than distinction has been advocated. This has often resulted in suspicion and even antagonism. Let us move into the new millennium with a re-united approach and realise again how all of the many and various 'fruit' come from the same tree 'trunk' as Wassily Kandinsky said nearly a hundred years ago: '*The mysterious and precious fact is that the fruit produced from the same trunk is different*'.

In order for you to gain maximum benefit from this book I urge you to read each page in turn and engage in all of the practical exercises as soon as they are presented to you. Treat the book as a progressive course. There are so many and various aspects of design that they cannot be presented all at once. Therefore read the book sequentially and consider the exercises as individual pieces of a jigsaw puzzle whose picture as a whole will gradually be revealed as you proceed towards the end of the book.

'*But what*', you may now well ask, '*is design? What does it really mean? And what does it involve?*'

There are a number of meanings for the word 'design' Although they are inseparable, they can be distinguished.

> '*Design means intention, motive and should as such be applied to the smallest as to the greatest efforts in art.*'
>
> *Lady Marion M. Alford.*

Let us begin by categorising these meanings under two headings. 'Content' and 'Process'. 'Content' has two sub-headings: 'Intention' and 'Composition'.

Design as Content

Firstly, there is design as content. The word, 'content' itself constitutes two other specific meanings which are integrated. These are design as intention and design as composition. The word, 'intention' refers to the purpose or reason for the created object and the word 'composition' refers to the form or materialisation of the object.

Design as Intention

Every object, small or great, has its intention, motive, reason and purpose. Such intentions can be extremely various and range from decorative, functional, descriptive, abstract, expressive and symbolic. Such intentions are the driving forces for all men and women engaged in all art and craft disciplines throughout all history and in all cultures. Furthermore, these intentions can manifest themselves either singly or more often combined in some way or other.

The delightful pincushion (Fig. 1) is decorative, functional and abstract; it represents nothing extrinsic from its own beauty. The collar for lingerie (Fig. 2) is also decorative and functional. However, the abstracted forms evoke our concepts of flowers and foliage. Fig. 3, entitled 'Touching Wood' is a detail of one of a series by Jean Littlejohn whose current work is both expressive and symbolic and contains references to myth, legend and superstition.

Thus these three very different pieces can help us to understand that every object is based upon an idea, however great or small, or a combination of several ideas, which when formed in the mind of the maker becomes the intention of the object. Once formed by the maker in material, and whose elements such as colours, textures and shapes are composed to create a coherent unity, the intention then becomes the content – the substance – of the object's form. As Ben Shahn said, *'Form is the embodiment of content'.*

Design as Composition

The word 'composition' refers to the act or art of putting together and forming an integrated unity. This presupposes that there must be some ingredients to be put together. These we can call the 'formal elements' such as colour, texture and shape because they are the elements that constitute the form. Composition also presupposes that there must be some systems by which these elements may be put together. Such systems we call 'compositional principles' such as repetition, contrast , complication and simplification. Composition presupposes yet one more consideration which leads us to the process of designing itself – our second main heading.

'The content of a work of art finds its expression in the composition.'

Wassily Kandinsky

Design as Process

The word 'process' refers to the ways and procedures by which an object can be made by employing all the powers of human creativity at our disposal. Our sensitivity to problems, our flexibility to situations, our fluency in skills and our originality in ideas and responses all affect the particular way we work as individuals; each one of us honestly and uniquely contributing to one enormous system of artistic communication, indeed, communion.

Such meanings of design and all their ramifications constitute the underlying substance of this book as a whole. However, in order to present them as clearly as possible, the book is constructed in four parts. Part One is this introduction which you are now reading. Part Two specifically addresses the formal elements of design such as colour, texture, point, line, direction, angle and shape. Part Three addresses the compositional principles of design such as unity, harmony, repetition, contrast, rhythm, alternation, symmetry, progression, gradation, proportion, complication and simplicity. Finally, Part Four addresses the process of designing itself and investigates such considerations as sensitivity, flexibility, fluency, originality and other such qualities which direct how we think and act; indeed, govern our very creative being.

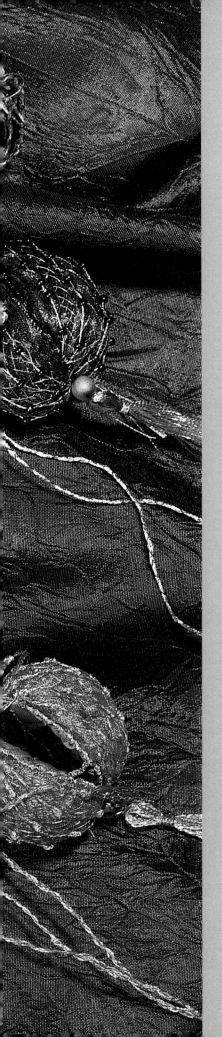

PART TWO

THE FORMAL ELEMENTS OF DESIGN

The formal elements which we shall now explore are colour, texture, point, line, direction, angle and shape. Experiment with the accompanying exercises as soon as they are presented to you. Intellectual understanding is dependant on practical experience. Therefore, avoid the temptation of reading too much in advance so that you do not impede the enjoyment of your journey. Work in a quiet and conducive environment free from distractions. Sit comfortably and spend a few minutes relaxing your body and allowing your mind to be free from extraneous thoughts. Even meditate for a while, so that your attention comes to the present and is prepared for the task ahead.

Colour

Are you captivated but confused by colour? If so, read the following paragraphs slowly and carefully. Take your time and engage in each exercise several times as if they were all new and exciting adventures. Do not worry if you do not succeed immediately. Be more encouraged that you have started your journey like professionals, who are still journeying through their adventures, and

like scientists, who have proposed many useful theories, yet know that they have not fully explained this amazing phenomenon of Nature.

Colour is probably the most immediately attractive of all the formal elements. Nature offers us enormous varieties and combinations of colours. Physical scientists as far back as Seneca, who held angular glass rods up to the light to produce a rainbow, have demonstrated that all colours are components of white light. All colours belong to each other and can harmonise with each other in our creations as they do in all manifestations in Nature.

Research has shown that we can distinguish between 120 and 200 individual colours. Maybe this explains why there are so many opinions about how many actual colours there are in the spectrum. Twelve, nine, seven and six have all been suggested. For the time being let us agree with there being just six main colours in the spectrum.

If you have never made a colour circle before, try your first main exercise now by emulating Fig. 4. Choose three coloured pencils. Select a purplish-blue such as ultramarine or royal blue which is like the blue of a cornflower, a purplish-red such as crimson which is like the red of ripe holly berries and an orangish-

yellow such as gamboge or cadmium yellow which is like the yellow of a buttercup. By mixing the primary colours of blue, red and yellow you will discover that you can make the secondary colours of green orange and purple. Follow the colour key at the outer rim of the colour circle in Fig. 4 to help you.

The colours which appear opposite to each other in this circle (red and green, yellow and purple, blue and orange) are known as complementary pairs. This knowledge and use of complementary colours is of utmost importance to all of us who design and which you can look forward to exploring as this book proceeds.

Look now at Fig. 5. It is one of a number of samples by Rosalind Floyd leading towards a large embroidery entitled 'Razzle Dazzle'. All the various illusions of orange, purple and green in the rectangles have been composed by subtle proportions and juxtapositions of just one yellow, one blue and one red. You could try such experiments yourself with coloured pencils and also with threads and see what happens.

Now make a twelve part colour circle as your second main exercise. Use the same three coloured pencils but also select three more. Include a greenish-blue like the blue of a turquoise, an orangish-red like scarlet and a greenish-yellow like the colour of a primrose or a not too ripe lemon. Follow the colour

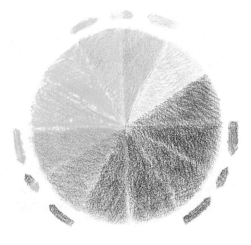

◀ **Fig 6** Twelve-part colour circle. Make the two different greens, purples and oranges by mixing hues of the two primary colours either side of the appropriate sectors. For example, the two greens are both made with just the greenish blue and the greenish yellow. Make the bluish green by mixing more blue with less yellow; make the yellowish green by mixing more yellow with less blue. Each pair of primary colours – and proportion – is shown at the outer rim of the circle and next to the curve of the appropriate sector.

key at the outer rim of the colour circle in Fig. 6 to help you.

The same manifestation of complementary colours is present as in the six-part circle but in a more specific form in this twelve-part circle. For example you can observe that the orangish hue of yellow is a direct complementary to the bluish hue of purple.

It has been generally agreed by those investigating the phenomenon of colour over many centuries that there are three inseparable but distinguishing characteristics. Some have also included a fourth. These are 'hue', 'tonal value', 'chromatic value' and 'temperature'.

Hue

Hue is a term which refers to the characteristic that distinguishes one particular colour from another such

as red from purple, purple from blue and so forth. This is its general meaning. Its more specific meaning distinguishes variations within the general. For example, a scarlet and a crimson are both red but a scarlet is an orangish hue of red and a crimson is a purplish hue of red. You have already observed this in your six coloured pencils and you have also made two hues of each of the three secondary colours in your second exercise.

Now prepare for the next three main exercises by selecting from a pile of coloured magazines parts of the page that are coloured with one general hue. Let us choose blue. Cut away about thirty or even forty different kinds of blue - the more the merrier!

For the first of these three main exercises select some of these blues and grade them so that you create a scale from purplish hues of blue right through to greenish hues of blue. Refer to Fig. 7 to help you. You could try some similar experiments with your

▶ **Fig 7** Scale of hues of blue.

▶ **Fig 9** Scale of tonal values of blue.

▲ **Fig 8** Hand-embroidered purses by Maureen King 1990s. Silk threads on silk fabric in a variety of hues, tones and chromatic values of red.

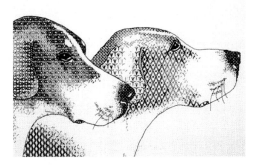

coloured pencils or with a range of threads or even a variety of fabrics by exploring a variety of hues within any one particular colour. Look now at Fig. 8 and notice the very subtle range of reds employed by Maureen King to embroider her exquisite purses.

Tonal Value

'Value', 'tone' and 'tonal value' are terms which all refer to the range (of any hue) between pale and dark. Now try the second of these three main exercises. Select some more pieces from your pile of magazine cuttings and grade them so you create a scale from very pale blue right through to dark blue. Sometimes the brightness and dullness of hues (our next characteristic for discussion) can beguile

our assessment of tonal values of hues. A useful way to check your attempt is to take a black and white photocopy of it. Refer to Fig. 9 to guide you. You could try similar experiments with an ordinary pen or pencil. Look at Figs 10, 11 and 12 to help you.

Tonal values of colour are essential to all design. Without them the images and forms would be visually incomprehensible. Look now at Fig. 13 and notice the range of tones from dark to pale blues and dark reds to pale reds, which we generally call 'pink', in the flowers, and dark to pale green in the leaves. Look now at Fig. 14 where the techniques of blackwork embroidery permit the range between sparse and dense stitching to create a variety of tonal values. Your engagement in exercises similar to those illustrated in Figs 11 and 12 will augment your understanding of this principle.

Chromatic Value

'Chroma', 'chromatic value', 'intensity', 'saturation' and 'purity' are terms which all refer to the range (of any hue) between bright and dull.

It is important to stress that bright colours need

◀ **Fig 14** 'Hounds' by Amanda Ewing 1933. Blackwork. From the Royal School of Needlework Collection. (Photograph: RSN.)

◀◀ **Fig 13** A detail of a 'Bouquet of Flowers' by Alice Jones 1912–1915. Silk shading. From the Royal School of Needlework collection. (Photograph: RSN.)

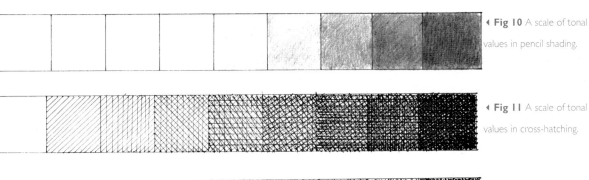

◀ **Fig 10** A scale of tonal values in pencil shading.

◀ **Fig 11** A scale of tonal values in cross-hatching.

◀ **Fig 12** A scale of tonal values in points and dots.

not necessarily appear brash and garish, nor do dull, muted and subdued colours always seem dreary and boring. The Delhi Shawl (Fig. 16) consists of much bright green and red. However, their juxtaposition with black simultaneously enhances and contains this quality. Most of the embroidered walnuts (Fig. 17), are dull coloured. However, they are exceptionally sumptuous because of the variety of tonal and textural contrasts. You will remember reading in the introduction that although certain meanings of design can be distinguished, they are also inseparable; the same applies to all of the formal elements.

When you have completed these three main exercises, look again at the illustrations (Figs. 7, 9 and 15) and notice that although one particular characteristic of colour has been graded in each scale, the other two characteristics are still present but placed arbitrarily. Is this so in your three exercises? We need to remember that although all three characteristics are integrated and inseparable, we are not yet trying to create a scale of all three characteristics in any one exercise.

Temperature

Many artists and designers have long designated certain colours as being warm and cool. This is not only psychologically but also physically true. A very sensitive thermometer called a thermopile registers a change in temperature when placed over different colours. Reds tend to be warmest and blues tend to be coolest physically. Look at your colour circles again to see that this is so. Look also at Figs 7, 9 and 15 again and notice how the purplish blues look the warmest of all the blues. Furthermore, notice how the greenish blues also look slightly warmer than purer blues. This is because of the marginal inclusion of yellow which is considered to be a warmish colour.

More Exercises in Hue, Tonal value, Chromatic value and Temperature

You could try some other exercises which will help you to clarify your understanding of these four characteristics of colour even more. Also try using a different medium such as paint. Figs 18 to 22 have all been painted with water-colours.

Figs 18 and 19 are scales of hues of blue. From left to right in both illustrations you will see how purplish blues progress to greenish blues with the extra distinction that the scale in Fig. 18 is of similar pale tones, and the scale in Fig. 19 is of similar dark tones. To perform both exercises choose a range of blues from your paint box and mix them so that the appropriate scales are achieved. You could even add a vestige of yellow to the greenish blue and a vestige of red to the purplish blue in order to extend the range of your scales. To achieve the pale tones mix a little pigment with a lot of water and vice-versa for the dark tones.

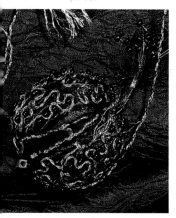

▼ **Fig 17** Detail of embroidered walnut shells by Maureen King 1990s (p 14). The concept derives from sixteenth century nut purses.

▶▶ **Fig 16** Delhi shawl. Early nineteenth century. Silk embroidery. From the Margaret Hall-Townley collection.

▶ **Fig 15** A scale of chromatic values of blue.

▶ **Fig 18** Scale of pale
   hues of blue.

▶ **Fig 19** Scale of dark
   hues of blue.

▶ **Fig 20** Tonal scale of
   one hue of blue.

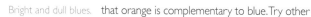

Fig. 20 is a tonal scale of just one hue of blue. Follow the same guide described at the end of the previous paragraph to achieve the range between pale and dark tonal values.

Fig. 21 is a diagram showing three hues of blue that are bright in the left vertical column, dull in the centre column and how this is achieved by laying a very pale wash of orange over the bright blues in the right column. As you try this yourself, you will realise that orange is complementary to blue. Try other variations of making any bright colour dull by mixing it with a small amount of its complementary colour.

▼ **Fig 21**

Bright and dull blues.

Simultaneous Contrast

Colour is always seen in relation to its surroundings and is always affected by them. This phenomenon is known as 'simultaneous contrast'. Hue, tonal value, chromatic value and temperature all change under different circumstances. Look at Fig. 22 and notice how the small blue squares appear different even though they have been painted with the same colour. Each appears to take on something of the opposite - and, therefore, the complementary and contrasting - characteristics of their surrounding colour. For examples - the small square surrounded by the darkest, dullest colour appears palest and brightest, the small square surrounded by the purplish, brightest and warmest colour looks greenish, dullest and coolest, and the small square surrounded by the palest, greenish and coolest colour appears darkest, reddish-purple and warmest.

Try making such diagrams yourself. As you do so, you will notice other differences, which you may have

◀ **Fig 22** Simultaneous contrast of blues.

seen already. For examples - the small square surrounded by the darkest colour seems larger than the others and appears to advance. Conversely, the small square surrounded by the palest colour seems smaller and appears to recede.

Such interactions have always been and shall probably always remain important devices for designers to create compositional emphasis. Later on you will discover how this applies not only to colour, which is exciting enough in itself, but also to all the other elements.

Colour Expression and Symbolism

Not only does colour have physical characteristics, which you have just begun to explore, it also has long been supposed to convey certain impressions on the mind. As a result the psychological characteristics of colour have been used expressively by individuals and have been systematised generally for symbolic

'Harmonies and concords of colours which are sufficient in themselves and which succeed in touching us to the depths of our being; without the aid of a more precise or clearly enunciated idea.'

Claude Monet.

purposes. In both instances these have varied from time to time, from culture to culture and from place to place.

Let us now investigate each colour in turn to note some generalisations but also to bear in mind that they are not exempt from subjective interpretations and are open to infinite extensions. We should also bear in mind that such interpretations and extensions are subject to how each colour is related to other colours and, as we have noticed before, to all the other formal elements. As you proceed through these investigations try some experiments similar to those you emulated earlier (Figs 7, 9, 15 and 18 to 22) and compare your responses to the colours with their descriptions that now follow.

Yellow

Yellow is the most light-giving of all hues. Yellows tending towards orange, (like gold) are, as Johannes Itten describes, *'The highest sublimation of matter by the power of light, impalpably radiant, lacking*

▶ **Fig 23** St Clement's Golden Cope 1870s. Made by Buckley and Co., and exhibited at the church congresses of 1880 and 1882. Described as the richest product in this country for the last three hundred years. The semi-circular placement of motifs was based on an arrangement typical of medieval copes. *'Such work'*, says May Morris, *'with its quality of mystery, had a living splendour, and was indeed "fit for Kings' treasuries" as the simple saying has it, or as we might say nowadays, fit to gladden the eyes of all who believe that everything beautiful that is made serves its due purpose in enriching the treasury of the world.'* From the Elizabeth Hoare collection housed in the Liverpool Cathedral Embroidery Museum. (Photograph: Ilse Richie).

transparency, but weightless as pure vibration'. Yellow, has long been recognised as the symbol of love, constancy, dignity and cheerfulness. It was the imperial colour in China - the celestial empire - and an orange-yellow is still the priestly colour of Buddhism. To describe someone as 'bright' is to acknowledge the person has intelligence. Therefore, yellow being the brightest hue has been symbolic of understanding, knowledge and wisdom. Because gold is incorruptible, and whose colour is yellow and glitters like the sun, it was much used in Byzantine mosaics, medieval and early Renaissance paintings to symbolise eternity, heavenly radiance and spiritual illumination. For the same reason, ever since the eleventh and twelfth centuries when *Opus Anglicanum* (English work)

> *'Yellow being the colour of the sun and of corn and gold, represents riches generosity and light'.*
>
> *Lady Marion M. Alford.*

was at its height, ecclesiastical vestments are still embroidered with gold threads. The St Clement's Golden Cope (Fig. 23) is a sumptuous example.

Many of our wild flowers are yellow, particularly in Spring. Although this colour might predominate in a bank of primroses and celandines, it is often accompanied with the purple of violets. The splendid sight of a field of buttercups is often enhanced by the inclusion of the pale mauve of lady's smock and the red-purple of clover.

I have used this pair of complementary colours in The Buttercup Field (Fig. 24). If you look carefully you will detect very small amounts of purple fabric and thread to augment the larger expanses of yellow. This way of using complementary colours is a useful device for all designers for compositional emphasis. We shall discuss

▲ Fig 24
'Buttercup Field' by the
author 1999. Fabric
collage with machine
and hand embroidery.

Blue

this further in Part Three but, in the meantime observe how Nature uses yellow with other colours, try some experiments and come to know what Sir Philip Sidney meant when he said 'There is no art delivered to mankind that hath not the works of Nature for his principle object.'

All yellows when pale and bright suggest purity and freshness. However when they become dark and dull they can symbolise reverse meanings. Such yellows are associated with sickness and disease; yellow flags were flown on quarantined ships and sometimes on hospitals. They also symbolise cowardice, deceit and treachery; doors on traitors' houses were painted yellow in tenth-century France and Judas has often been represented in yellow attire. Try experimenting with dull and dark yellows and observe your own reactions to these colours compared to the reactions you have to pale and bright yellows.

'Among the Mayas blue, being the colour of the vault of heaven, was symbolic of holiness, sanctity, chastity, hence of happiness. In Mexico, Egypt and Chaldea, blue was worn during mourning as a token of the felicity, which the soul, freed from the trammels of matter, was enjoying in the celestial regions.'

Harold Bayley

In nearly all societies throughout the world blues express purity, peace and passivity. 'They are cold', as Goethe describes, 'they disembody, and they evoke impressions of expanse and distance, and boundless – enchanting nothingness.' Blues recall the distant sky, the calm ocean and have immortal and celestial characters. In some cultures blues are used to create an environment for meditation. Within the Christian church blues signify sincerity, hope and serenity. Although Itten describes dimmed and darkened blues falling into 'superstition, fear, grief and perdition' he goes on to say that they 'always point to the realm of the transcendental.' To create this transcendental effect Verina Warren has used these kinds of blues in her mysteriously magnificent work entitled 'Bless The Lord All Created Things' (Fig. 25) which is one of a series based on The Song of Creation, from the Prayer Book.

The term 'blue-blooded'

▶ **Fig 25** 'Bless The Lord All Created Things' by Verina Warren 1998. Painting, air-brushing and embroidery on silk. 'Initially, I had difficulty achieving the density of colour I wanted on the background, as I wanted to fade it towards the central arch. I needed a blue-blackness, with a hint of purple to get the colour I required. This was essential as I needed that density in order to create the effect of the "world" hanging suspended in space and time. After much colour mixing and air-brushing I finally achieved the effect I wanted.' (Photograph: Verina Warren).

denotes aristocracy which may originate as far back as three thousand years ago when Egyptians painted their gods blue in order to signify their exalted and heavenly character. For the Chinese it symbolised immortality and the Aztecs offered themselves as propitiatory sacrifices to their deity smeared with blue paint.

As you have already carried out a number of exercises using just blue, try some others in which you juxtapose blue with other colours. Blue with yellow is an interesting combination. Because both colours have similar significance they have often been used together for similar spiritual purposes to express and symbolise the mysterious, the magnificent and the marvellous. Look at Fig. 26 entitled, 'Bless The Lord All Ye Birds Of The Air' by Verina Warren, which is another in the same series as Fig. 25. Here you will see a border of bright yellow surrounding the central section of blue descending to green over which the birds, mainly blue in colour, move in a spiral. Read now her own words as she describes her intentions and how she creates a harmonious balance. 'Although the border is lively with the interpretation of the birds and the essence of flight, I also wanted to achieve an inner calm, which if you look into the garden, beyond the three birds immediately below the circle, there is a depth of mystery and indeed within the circle itself, an inner stillness. The balance had worked.'

Red

Red is extraordinarily flexible and can convey many diverse characteristics depending on its hue, tone and saturation. Red has a strong committed

▲ **Fig 26** 'Bless The Lord All Ye Birds of the Air,' Verina Warren 1998. Painting, air-brushing and embroidery on silk. 'As I wanted something bright and full of life, yellow was an obvious choice of colour, so I decided to use this for the background. I air-brushed a piece of antung silk, shading the colour from dark orange- yellow at the base, lightening towards the top, especially around the circle which represents eternity, creation, without beginning or end. The central section was also air-brushed from yellow-greens to blues, and then this was applied to the yellow base. As this was to portray the essence of a mystical garden, perhaps even the Garden of Eden, I wanted it to be precisely defined and the yellow tones against the blue visually emphasised this definition. The birds were mainly painted in blues, greens and browns to represent earth and sky. They are also placed in the form of a spiral to give a sense of movement. Within Celtic symbolism the spiral has many deep religious connotations thus giving inner meaning to this work.' (Photograph: Verina Warren).

character and is associated with passionate actions. It is the colour of blood and associated with life, love and sex. Who has not received a bouquet of red roses on St Valentine's Day and not known that they were a token of love? In many oriental countries, such as India or China, red is used in connection with the marriage ceremony. Fig. 27 is a wedding dress, called a *Kamise*, and comes from the region of mountains and valleys in Pakistan; its colour is not only a celebration of sex but also used to ward off evil spirits. In occidental countries, terms like 'scarlet woman' and 'the red light districts' are also allusions to the sexual aspect of this colour but with reverse ('naughty') connotations.

Generally, purplish hues of red are associated with spiritual love whereas orangish hues of red are associated with physical love, but also with hate and are often used to express feverish, even belligerent, passion. However, both reds can interchange their roles depending on their juxtaposition with other colours. Allied to the planet Mars, named after the Roman god of war, red has been used to express strife, conflict and battle. Jan Beaney uses much bright red in her dramatic embroidery entitled 'A Beautiful but Troubled Lane' (Fig. 28) to express tense feelings. She describes the work in the following words, 'This piece was inspired by a journey

'Of all the colours red has the strongest chroma and the greatest power of attraction. It is positive, aggressive and exciting.'

Maitland Graves.

through Israel where the scenery and atmosphere aroused unexpected emotions. The strongly coloured images within the varying landscapes are combined with crosses and diagonals to depict the tensions, divisions and barriers experienced in this historic land.'

The Christian church uses red variously. On one hand, the red-hot fires of hell seething with red devils are expressive of eternal damnation. On the other hand, red signifies the holy blood of Christ, the sacrifice of martyrs and Pentecostal flames are expressive of eternal salvation.

When red is pale, which we generally call pink, it assumes a more restful, serene and gentle character, as you have probably already noticed where it appears in Fig. 8 and 13.

Thus red can be positively uplifting or negatively

▲ **Fig 27** A *Kamise*, a wedding dress from Pakistan 1930s. The design derives from ancient traditions. The red colour and certain motifs are used to ward off the *djinn* - the evil spirits in Muslim mythology. From the Margaret Hall-Townley collection.

Green

Green combines the radiance of yellow and the coolness of blue. Fruitfulness, contentment and tranquillity are all expressive values of green. Kandinsky wrote, '*On exhausted men this restfulness has a beneficial effect, but after a time it can become wearisome.*' We have already noticed how a great expanse of any one colour viewed for a long time can be 'wearisome'. No one colour exists on its own in Nature. Look at Fig. 29 illustrating a landscape with trees and ferns and observe how Alison Holt juxtaposes green with a reddish brown, which is essentially a dark, dull red and, therefore complementary to green. She writes of her work, '*My intention is to represent the atmosphere and strong visual elements that attract me. My work is concerned with a sense of light and interesting juxtapositions of colour, shape and textures I find in gardens and landscapes.*'

In Christian liturgy, green represents faith, immortality and contemplation. Look again at Fig. 26 and notice once more how green is used with yellow and blue to create an inner stillness.

Try some exercises using green on its own and with other colours and watch your own reactions to the variations you create.

▲ **Fig 29**
Woodland Ferns by Alison Holt 1998. Machine embroidery with painted elements. (Photograph: Myk Briggs).

destructive. As Itten describes, '*It can be widely varied between warm and cold, dull and clear, light and dark, without destroying the character of redness. From demonic, sinister red-orange on black, to sweet angelic pink, red can express all intermediate degrees between the infernal and the sublime.*'

Now try a few experiments with red but avoid staying too long with any one of these exercises at a time lest you 'see red'! Its positive character is generally realised in small amounts and for a short time. Otherwise it can become particularly aggressive.

▸▸ **Fig 28** 'A Beautiful but Troubled Lane' by Jan Beaney 1998. Fragments of cloth assembled from applied fabrics, plastics, mixed media and machine-embroidered on soluble material with hand stitches.

'*Green universally symbolises growth, expressing fertility and the yearly renewal of plant life on the earth. It has been called the colour of "elastic tension" conveying the qualties of both energy and eveness that are present in its component of yellow and blue.*'

Carolyn M. Bloomer

Orange

Orange, like red is generally warm, positive and exciting. It is thought to be a proud colour and sometimes even ostentatious. Like yellow and red, which constitute it, orange is often associated with the colour of autumn leaves, which in the last stages of their lives, assert their existence like flames. The splendid rug by Ann Davies (Fig. 30) positively sizzles. It will come as no surprise to you that her design originates from the fiery colours of the Virginia creeper during the later months of the year.

Like most colours, when pale in tone, orange has a more gentle character which you can observe ahead in fig. 62 illustrating a detail of a tablecloth whose border depicts nasturtiums embroidered by Rosemary Tindall in the 1930s.

Copper's colour is orange. Maureen King has used a small sheet of this metal as a mirror and employed orange and blue as the colours for its felted and embroidered frame and covering. This exquisite piece (Fig. 31) is a perfect example of how complementaries can be used effectively. As Charles Blanc said, 'Let the complementary colour be its auxiliary and not its rival… if contrast is needed let it be used as rendering the whole more powerful, brilliant and striking.' Here orange attracts our attention and dominates the decoration. However, it is used sparingly – the 'auxiliary' not the 'rival' to the larger amount of blue. In many situations it is the minority rather then the majority that is the more conspicuous. This precept is of fundamental importance for all designers to create focuses of interest. Furthermore Maureen King has allowed both colours to mingle in some areas, as she dyed the felt, so that the muted mixtures enhance the singletons. You will remember how you made such mixtures of dull and muted colours if you refer back to Fig. 21. Finally these dull areas are saved from tedium by their being embroidered with narrow braids and tiny glittering beads of both colours in bright and cheerful hues.

Explore orange yourself by trying some exercises. Juxtapose it and mix it with other colours, particularly with its complementary blue, and observe your responses.

◄◄ **Fig 30** 'Virginia Creeper' by Ann Davies 1998. Prodded rag-rug technique. The 'thrums' are made from old blankets dyed in the microwave.

▼ **Fig 31** 'Mirror and Case' by Maureen King 1997. Silk-embroidered felt. Embellished with braids and beads.

'Orange, the mixture of yellow and red, is at the focus of maximum radiant activity.'

Johannes Itten

Violet and Purple

The words violet and purple are in general speech interchangeable. Lady Marion Alford writes, *'the word purple is so indiscriminately used as a poetic epithet, rather than a distinctive appellation, that much confusion has been caused by it.'* Strictly speaking, violet tends towards blue and purple towards red. Violet, like blue, is cool and retiring but more subdued and withdrawn. It is used for the solemn seasons of Lent and Advent in the Christian Church and in China it was used for mourning. It is also used to create the effect of time and space. Look again at Fig. 25 which is Verina Warren's 'Bless the Lord All Created Things'. The dark blue is actually on the cusp between blue and violet which we call indigo in the rainbow. She admits to adding purple to the blue to achieve a blue-violet blackness. *'This was essential as I needed that density in order to create the effect of the "world" hanging suspended in space and time.'* Purple is stately, rich and impressive. It is the colour of royalty and favoured by ancient kings and emperors. The Latin word 'purpura' came to refer to a reddish-purple velvet which was dyed with a substance from shell-fish. Although Pliny praised the colour for its distinction he went on to say, *'Let us be prepared to excuse the frantic passion for purple, though we are impelled to inquire why such a high value is placed on the product of this fish, seeing that in the dye the smell of it is offensive'!*

In excess both violet and purple can be oppressive and morbid. Look at Fig. 32 which is another of Maureen King's gorgeously rich purses. The prevention of oppression and morbidity is achieved by the inclusion of blue with her use of both violet and purple. Both blue and red are components of violet and purple all of which have been used as the coloured threads to create the flower petals in the 'Jackmanii *Clematis*' canvas embroidery (Fig. 33). The inclusion of the two primary colours which constitute the secondary is of enormous use to designers. The device helps to enliven the colour and animates what could otherwise be tedious and wearisome.

Now try some exercises with violet and purple and include passages of red and blue in others

> 'Violet is often associated with mysticism and fantasy. Environmentally it is the colour of increasing distance and space. Violet, composed of red and blue, is subject to wide variation in hue and can seem either warm or cool, depending on its dominant component.'
>
> *Carolyn. M. Bloomer.*

▼ ▶▶ **Fig 32** Purse embroidered with grapes by Maureen King 1998. Detached button hole stitch in silk threads on silk fabric.

▸ **Fig 33**
'Jackmanii Clematis'
designed by the author.
Embroidered by
Christine Lund 1998.
Computer realisation by
Andrew Lund. Half
cross-stitch canvas
embroidery in
tapestry wools.

Brown

and compare the differences. Return also to green and orange and try similar experiments. Remember to avoid looking at looking at large areas of any one colour for a long time, particularly violet. Itten said 'It can be distinctly terrifying' and Goethe said, 'A light of this kind suggests the terrors of the end of the world.'

▸▸ Fig 34 Goldwork Circle from India. Late nineteenth century. From the Royal School of Needlework Collection. (Photograph: RSN).

'Brown is unemotional and disciplined.It is outwardly inaudible but rings of a powerful inner harmony.'

Wassily Kandinsky

Browns are actually dark dull reds, yellows, oranges and a very dull green. For convenience and ease in our daily lives we group them under this heading. However, we as designers, need to be less vague and more precise and specific to avoid confusion.

Brown is the colour of

the earth and can appear rich, fertile and comforting. Conversely it is also the colour of dirt, filth and mire and thus can appear repellent. As with all colours it depends entirely how it is juxtaposed.

Refer back to three illustrations. Firstly, look at Alison Holt's 'Woodland Ferns' (Fig. 29) and you will see that her use of red-brown is rich and warm because of its relationship with green. Secondly, look at Ann Davies' rug (Fig. 30) and notice both red-brown and orange-brown are included with bright yellows, oranges and dark reds. Finally, look at the 'Jackmanii *Clematis*' embroidery (Fig. 33) to see how the flowers are intensified by the surrounding dull yellow ochres. Now look at 'The Indian Gold work Circle' (Fig. 34) and notice that, although we understand that we are looking at gold we actually perceive many, but very small amounts of very pale yellow and a vast quantity of very dark, dull yellow, which we call 'brown'.

When we look about ourselves at our environment, browns – dark, dull reds, yellows, oranges and green – can be seen in abundance. They are the foils to all the brighter purer colours which we have been investigating. Bright colours may sit on 'thrones' but browns are the 'powers' behind them! The same can be said for greys and indeed for whites and blacks all of which we shall explore very soon. However first engage in some exercises with brown.

Using your coloured pencils or water-colours try making browns by mixing all three primaries together in different proportions. You could try the same process by mixing pairs of

complementaries. Refer back to Fig. 3 and notice how Jean Littlejohn has put tiny stitches of orange-yellow and blue-mauve threads into the dark, dull and muted green material which gives the overall effect of brown. Try experimenting now with fabric and threads in whatever techniques you like and observe what happens. A preponderance of warm colours will always produce brown, whereas a preponderance of cool colours generally produce the illusion of grey, which is one of the next colours for our examination.

White, Black and Grey

It could be argued that white, black and grey are strictly speaking, like brown, not colours of themselves but variations of other colours. Nevertheless, because they are capable of inducing moods and impressions on our minds, they are included here.

In a limited sense, these three can be considered as one colour hue with a vast range of tonal values. What colour is silver? It is white when caught by the light, black in dark shadow and grey between the two extremes. Look ahead to Fig. 106 which illustrates the Royal Coat of Arms and in particular to the silver unicorn and mantle to see that this is so. In a more expansive

'White is positive and stimulating, as compared with grey or black. It is luminous, airy, light and delicate.'

Maitland Graves

White

White, in western countries, has denoted purity, chastity, innocence and truth and is associated with weddings, christenings and confirmation ceremonies. However, in India and China it is used for mourning. The purity of white snowdrops in vast drifts is a wonderful sight as you can see in Alison Holt's embroidery (Fig. 35).

◄ **Fig 35**

'Snowdrops at Chirk Castle' by Alison Holt 1998.

Machine embroidery with painted elements.

(Photograph: Myk Briggs).

Black

As black is the opposite of white it has been identified with witchcraft and necromancy since pre-Christian times. Devil worship is known as 'The black art'. Nevertheless, there have been alternatives; Artemis, the Greek goddess of the moon has been represented as wearing both black and white and the Egyptian goddess Isis was depicted all in black expressing good significance. In western countries, black is worn for mourning to signify death and express grief. The black collar, a detail of which is illustrated in Fig. 39 would probably have been worn by a Victorian lady at such a time. Black is also symbolic of dignity as evinced by

sense, white can be considered as any colour of the palest possible tone (when we look at all of our so-called white fabrics and threads they all tend towards one of the six main colours of the colour circle [Fig. 4]) and black can be considered as any of the colours of the darkest possible tone (when we wash black clothes, we have observed how they exude various colours in the rinsing). Whereas browns tend to be warm, greys tend to have a cool cast. Now look at the central column in Fig. 21 and notice how the dull blues could be termed as grey. Have you noticed that dust in vacuum cleaners, fluff in tumble dryers and coloured strips of Plasticine, when mixed together, are all grey?

'Black is now the symbol of evil, but evidently it had originally a good signification.'

Harold Bayley.

the wearing of the colour by Christian priests and Spanish grandees. Black and white together is very striking which you can observe in Fig. 38 where the embroidered white flowers for appliqué have been laid on black velvet.

Colours next to black resound. Look back to Fig.

►**Fig 36** Pole fire-screens 1860. Berlin wool work with beads. From the Royal School of Needlework Collection. (Photograph: RSN.).

▶ **Fig 37** 'Moon and Stars' by Margaret Hall-Townley 1989. Embroidered with various hand stitches.

16 at the Delhi shawl and now look at the Victorian pole fire-screens (Fig 36) and notice how the colours glow because of their juxtaposition with black.

Grey

'A blend of black and white produces grey, which is silent and motionless.'

Wassily Kandinsky.

Some greys have a mellow richness and can be restful, pleasing and yield slight movement which is exemplified in Margaret Hall-Townley's 'Moon and Stars' (Fig. 37). Greys are use to express the vast impersonal phenomena of the cosmos but the nebulous forms such as light, space and air are interpreted in human terms because of the artist's belief that the movements in the universe also happen here on earth. The tall woman on the left represents the moon and is symbolic of the archetypal mother figure. She protects the stars which are depicted on the right as one hermaphrodite figure representative of all human kind. Subdued light, reflecting and emerging through light is achieved by the low relief elements of the piece and by the various kinds of intricate embroidery stitches.

Now try some experiments with blacks, whites and greys. A useful exercise is to make a collage of magazine cuttings, scraps of materials and lengths of threads in any one of these colours in order to notice how all of these substances are 'coloured' differently. Try as many exercises as you like so that you become more and more aware of their possibilities for your use.

We move now from this field of colour expression and symbolism. Remember that the descriptions you have just read are open to infinite extensions. Furthermore, not only colour but also such elements as texture, point, line, angle, shape and their concomitant areas, sizes, lengths, amounts and juxtapositions seem to convey impressions to the mind and therefore can be used expressively. Read on and discover this for yourself; you have many treats yet in store!

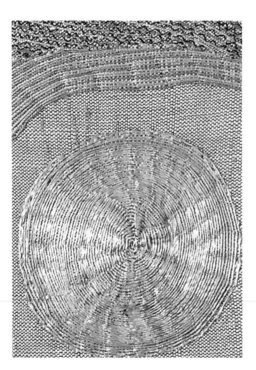

Texture

Texture is a significant element to all forms of art and craft but especially so in textiles. It is a

◀ **Fig 39**

Black Collar (Detail).
Late Victorian. Black
cotton twill edged with
Russian braid and
applied onto cotton net
by hand. Private
collection.

tactile element primarily received through the sense of touch. Warm, cool, rough, smooth, soft and hard textures need to be touched in order to be fully appreciated. Nevertheless, textures can be understood by sight because of certain visual clues. Wet, smooth and shiny surfaces reflect a greater tonal range between pale and dark colours than those that are dry, rough and matt. Furthermore, not only are tonal values of colour affected by texture but also are hues of colour and, to a certain extent, the chromatic values and temperatures of colour. Because texture affects light reflection and absorption, texture and colour are directly related.

Texture can also be used expressively as exemplified by the Sindhi wedding dress from the desert regions of Pakistan, the front of which is illustrated in Fig. 40. It is heavily encrusted with embroidery in very formal geometric patterns, almost like armour, as a form of protection against evil. The inclusion of little mirror glasses, metal spangles and gelatine sequins reflect, and therefore repel, wicked spirits. When the marriage has been solemnly pronounced, the bride reverses the dress so that the side with less formally designed embroidery is displayed as you see illustrated in Fig. 41.

Prepare now for your next series of

exercises. Spend some time collecting materials with different textural qualities such as various papers and plastics, types of card and packaging, metal foil and all kinds of fabric scraps. Make a collage in which you contrast rough with smooth and shiny with matt surfaces. Refer to Fig. 44 to help you. Notice in the illustration how the metal foil and the fabric composed of metallic threads reflect, like mirrors, a wide range of tonal values as well as the hues, chromatic values and temperatures of their surroundings.

Now select from your various materials with contrasting textures all those that are white. Dye them one hue of one colour and make another collage so that you may observe how texture affects all four characteristics of colour in spite of your initially limiting the range of both tonal values and hue. You will see in Fig. 43 this variety, even though the materials were once - surprisingly - all the same pale, white colour.

In addition to actual textures, there are those that are artificial or simulated. Try now some simulated textures like those you see illustrated in Fig. 42. Take a sheet of paper and cover it with a variety of artificial textures by such means as cross-

'Texture is the rendering of a surface. There is characteristic surface to all form, and this is as important as its structure.'

Andrew Loomis

hatching with a pen, stippling with a brush, dabbing with a sponge, rubbing a pencil onto paper placed over a textured surface, spattering with an old toothbrush and any other means that occurs to you.

Colours and textures may not exist alone; they cannot dispense themselves without boundaries. Such boundaries we call shapes. Shapes have contours and edges which we call lines. But before the line, there is the point, which we shall now explore.

◀◀ **Fig 40**

Sindhi wedding dress for merchant's daughter. Early twentieth century. From desert regions of Pakistan. Solid hand embroidery. From the Margaret Hall-Townley collection.

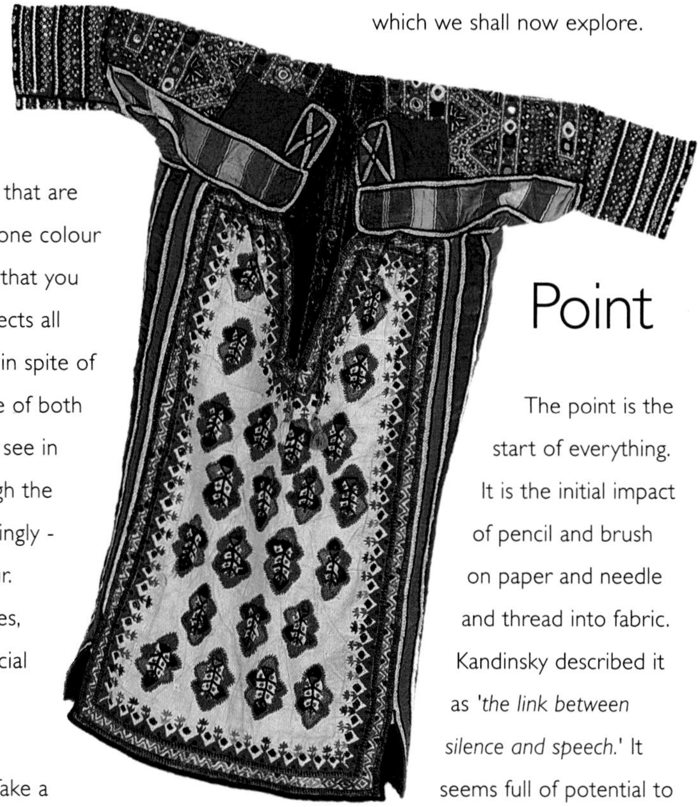

◀ **Fig 41**

Reverse side of the Sindhi wedding dress.

Point

The point is the start of everything. It is the initial impact of pencil and brush on paper and needle and thread into fabric. Kandinsky described it as *'the link between silence and speech.'* It seems full of potential to be anything it wants to be but on its own it remains the most restrained form. When

49

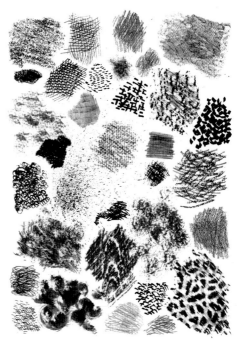

▸▸ Fig 42

Simulated textures.

▸ Fig 43

Collage with variously
textured white fabrics
all dyed the same
green.

▸▸ Fig 44

Collage with variously
textured surfaces.

juxtaposed with other points, 'pathways' and
different 'configurations' and 'sensations' result.
Some art and craft
forms are composed
entirely of points such as
pointillistic paintings,
mosaics, beadwork and
cross stitch
embroideries. The
Victorian pole fire-
screens (Fig. 36) are
sumptuous examples of
Berlin woolwork which
incorporate full cross
stitch. The cushion
representing 'The
Poppies' (Fig. 45) and
the 'Jackmanii *Clematis*'
(Fig. 33) are examples of
half-cross stitch.

*'The point may be used sim-
ply to identify or define a
position or positions - but as
the eye moves from one point
to another along different
visual pathways different
configurations and sensa-
tions result.'*

Frederick Malins

Many designs and compositions have centres of
interest or focal points. If you look at Fig. 47, which
is a diagram showing the
focal points for the
cushion (Fig. 45), you will
see how the areas of red
with dark centres lead our
eyes around the
composition. Now look at
Fig. 46, which is a diagram
showing just the one focal
point for Fig. 33, and you
will notice how your eyes
are drawn to just one
focal point located at the
yellow centre of the main
purple *clematis*. Other
designs, depending on
their intentions, need not
necessarily have any

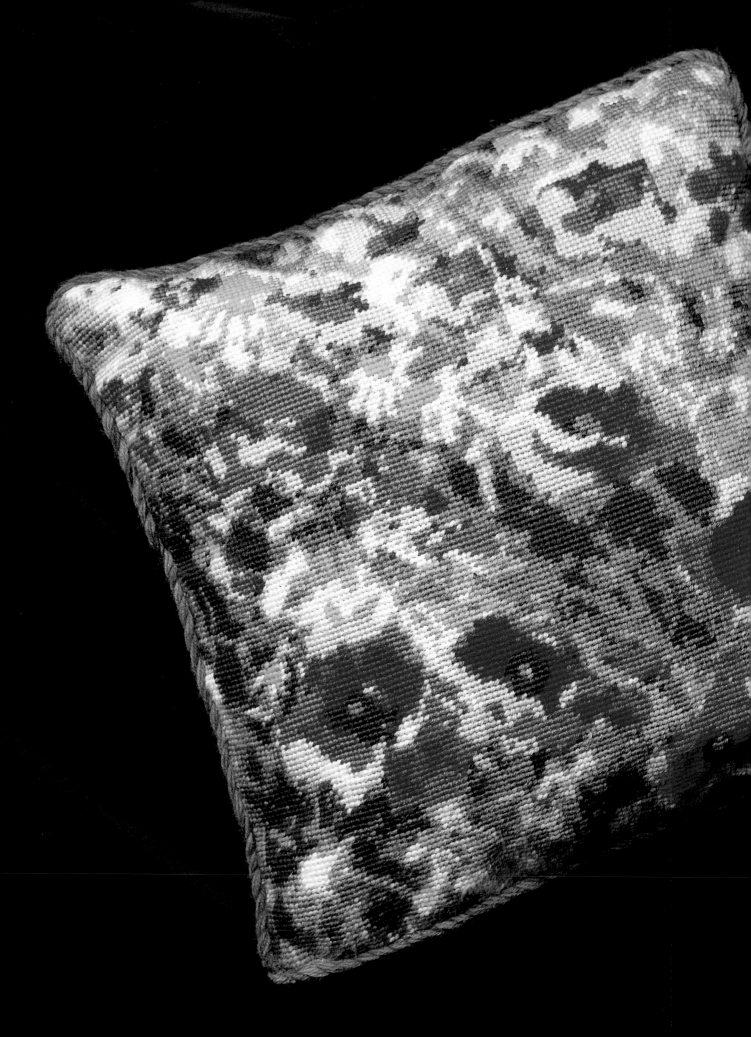

◄ **Fig 46** Focal point in 'The Jackmanii *Clematis*' (fig 33).

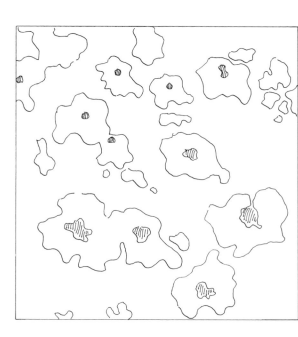

◄ **Fig 47**
Focal points in 'The Poppies' (fig 45).

◄◄ **Fig 45**
'The Poppies'. Designed by the author, computer realisation by Andrew Lund and embroidered by Christine Lund 1999. Half-cross stitch canvas embroidery in tapestry wools.

53

obvious focal points. Look back to Fig. 2, illustrating a collar for lingerie, and ahead to Fig. 52, illustrating a rug in horizontal lines, and you will notice that your eyes are not so much drawn to any one or more particular points but rather across the design as a whole.

Prepare now for your next series of exercises. Draw a number of rectangles on to a sheet of paper as you see in Fig. 48 and photocopy it a number of times. Clip one of these photocopied sheets on to the top edge of a drawing board, which could be a well-sanded off-cut of plywood. Take up a pen or pencil and sit comfortably with the lower edge of your drawing board in your lap and its upper edge resting on the edge of your work table. Without pause or hesitation place points or dots of various sizes in different positions and amounts into each rectangle. Take no more than a few minutes to complete the whole sheet. Refer to Fig. 49 to help you. Although testing and evaluating what we do is important, avoid engaging in criticism or judgement until you have completed this, and better still, several other sheets, so that you do not stem the flow of your creative imagination. Assessment of propriety and relevance can be delayed for a while.

'There are lines which travel fast...There are lines that are heavy, lines that have pain and lines that laugh. A line may plunge you into silences, with obscurity, and may bring you out into noise and clarity.'

Robert Henri

Line

Line is the point in motion. Force creates its mark. Its path can convey thoughts or actions whether it is straight or curved. As colours can convey moods to the mind so lines can suggest similar feelings. Straight lines suggest precision, seem positive and appear direct. Curved lines suggest flexibility, seem flowing and appear sensuous. Look at the diagrams illustrated by Figs 50a. and b. to see that this is so, and look at Fig. 53 which illustrates 'Punto in Aria' by Paddy Killer and notice how curved lines are particularly sensual. Now look at Fig. 51 which is a diagram showing the design composed substantially of horizontal lines in Ann Davies' rug (Fig. 52). Horizontals take preference but they are relieved by the tiny verticals where the colours change. Look carefully at Fig. 52 and notice the enormous variety within this simple format. Now compare your response to this design of horizontals and verticals with that composed entirely of curved lines in Fig. 54. This is a diagram for 'The Peacocks' (Fig. 67) which is a much faded, but still beautiful example of late nineteenth-century 'art needlework' which was rescued by its present owner from behind a dustbin!

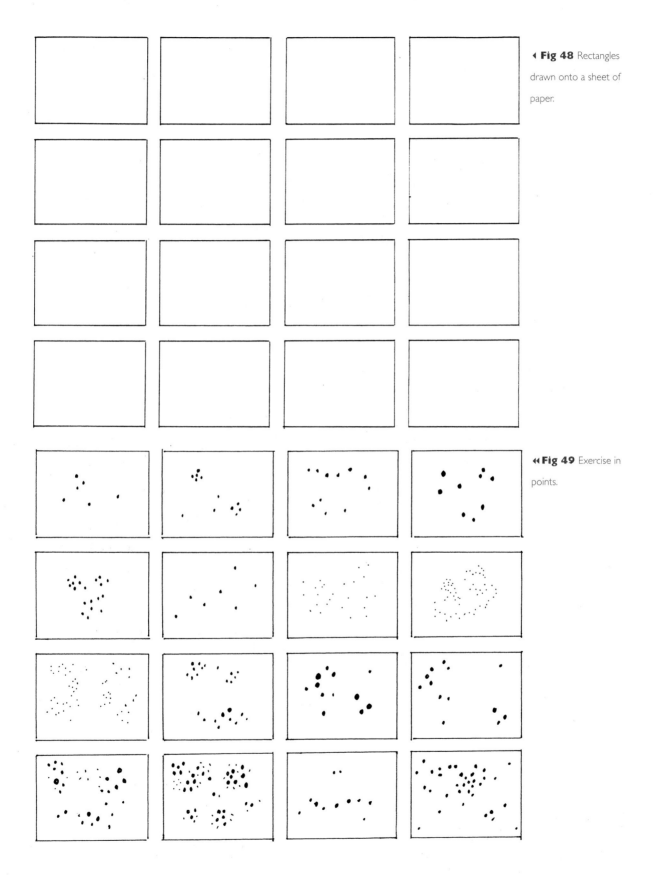

◄ **Fig 48** Rectangles drawn onto a sheet of paper.

◄◄ **Fig 49** Exercise in points.

◄ Fig 50(a) Straight
lines.

◄ Fig 50(b) Curved
lines.

▼ Fig 51 Diagram of
horizontal format of
lines composing the
design for the hooked
rug (fig 52).

◄◄ Fig 52
Hooked rug by
Ann Davies 1998.
Randomly dyed strips of
silk hooked into hessian.

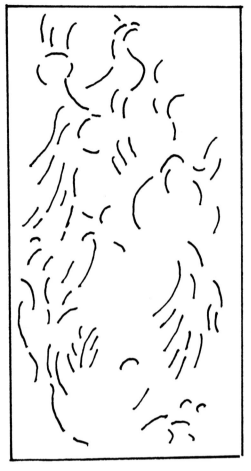

▶ Fig 54

Diagram of curved lines composing the design for 'The Peacocks' (fig. 67).

◄◄ Fig 53

'Punto in Aria' by Paddy Killer. A quilt based upon various representations of 'The Feasts of the Gods'. Drawn with Rotring pens onto satin, painted with fabric paints, free straight machine stitching. From the collection of the Embroiderers' Guild. (Photograph: Paddy Killer).

Direction

Look at the diagrams illustrated in Figs 55 to 58. Horizontals, which lie recumbent, seem restful, quiet and serene. Verticals, which stand upright, seem alert awake and dignified. Oblique lines, which lie at a slant, suggest motion and dynamism. Their movements can vary according to their degrees of inclination. Curved lines, by their very nature, gradate from one direction to another. Horizontals and verticals seem self-sufficient. Look again at the design of long horizontals (Fig. 51) together with short verticals (Fig. 52) of Ann Davies' rug and notice its completeness. Oblique lines can seem

insecure. However they can be supported by their relationship with other lines and their position in the composition. Now look back at Alison Holt's 'Woodland Ferns' (Fig. 29) and at Fig. 59, which is a diagram showing the main lines of the composition. You will notice how the oblique line representing the slanting tree on the right gives movement to the composition and how this is supported by other oblique lines in the opposite directions representing branches and trunks of trees on the left and the inclination of the brown earth, foliage and ferns (Fig. 60). You will also notice how the vertical lines representing most of the other trees are secure of themselves (Fig. 61) and when composed with the oblique lines (Fig. 59) give stability to the design. Curved lines can also seem insecure and, like horizontals, need support. Equilibrium is achieved in the design for 'The Peacocks' (Figs 54 and 67) by the complementary positions of the various curves throughout the composition.

Prepare now for some more exercises. Take four more sheets on which you have drawn rectangles and clip one for each exercise on your drawing board. Before you begin, read the remainder of this paragraph and the next two

'All lines have direction – horizontal, vertical and oblique. It is well known that each direction has a distinct and different effect upon the observer.'

Maitland Graves

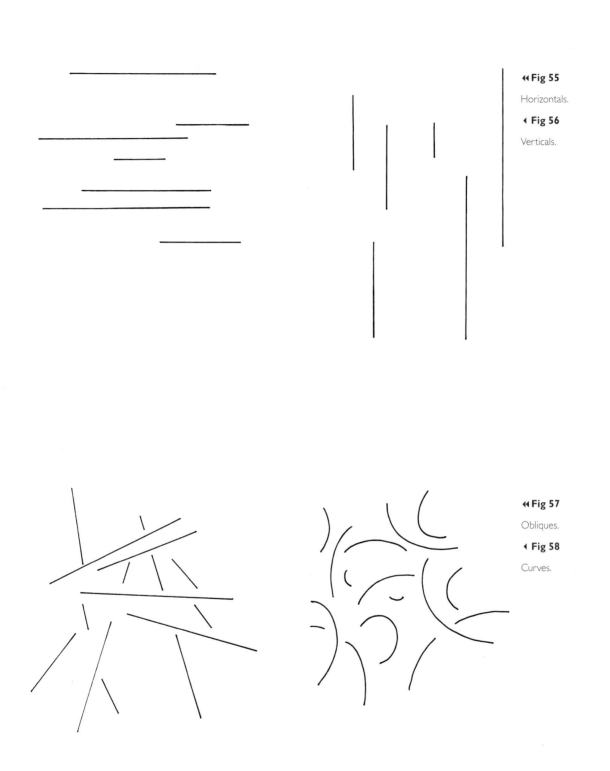

◀◀ **Fig 55**

Horizontals.

◀ **Fig 56**

Verticals.

◀◀ **Fig 57**

Obliques.

◀ **Fig 58**

Curves.

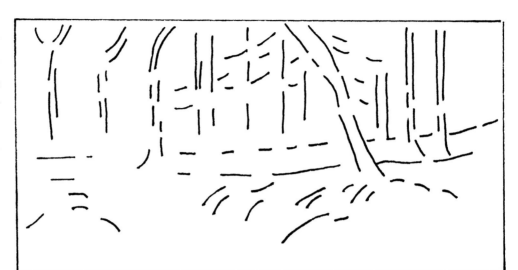

▶ Fig 59

Diagram of oblique and
vertical lines composing
the design for
'Woodland Ferns'
(fig. 29).

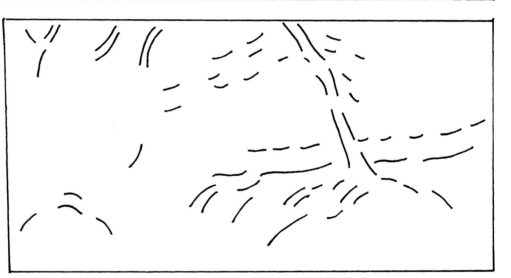

▶ Fig 60

Diagram of just the
oblique lines
in the design for
'Woodland Ferns'
(Fig. 29).

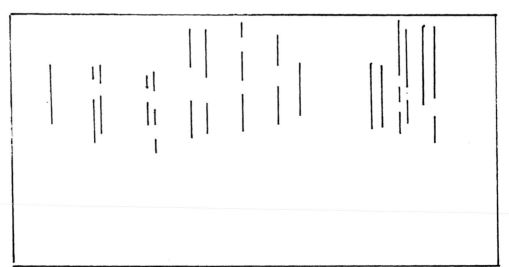

▶ Fig 61

Diagram of just the
vertical lines in the
design for
'Woodland Ferns'
(Fig. 29).

◄ **Fig 62** Nasturtiums.
Detail of a tablecloth
embroidered in satin
stitch and Russian filling
stitch by Rosemary
Tindall 1930s.
Note how the curves
are stabilised by the
straight horizontal and
vertical lines in the
design.

sections headed 'Angle' and 'Shape'. Complete one sheet with horizontals, a second with verticals, a third with oblique lines and a fourth with curves. Vary their lengths, amounts and positions within each rectangle on every sheet. Look ahead to the examples shown in Figs 68 to 71 and notice that some lines are long, others short. In some rectangles there are only a few lines, in others there are many. 'Variety' it has been said, 'is the spice of life'.

'As lines, so loves oblique, may well

Themselves in every angle greet:

But ours so truly parallel,

Though infinite, can never meet.'

Andrew Marvell

appears open to suggestion (Fig. 65). Repeated angles in one movement create a zigzagging line whose agitation suggests energy and excitement like forked lightning (Fig. 66).

Angle

If you should allow the oblique lines (on your third sheet) to meet or overlap you will form angles, as you see in some of those illustrated in Fig. 70. You could even contrive to create the three types of angles that geometricians have identified. Angles, like other elements are capable of conveying feelings. A right angle seems stable, and if not placed at a slant, appears still (Fig. 63). The acute, like an arrow, seems active and fast (Fig. 64). The obtuse (or reflex) angle gently combines the characteristics of the other two angles and

'Rectilinear shapes and curvilinear shapes appear to have differing potentials in terms of suggesting movement.'

Maurice de Sausmarez

Shape

As you experiment with more angles on this sheet with oblique lines (Fig. 70), you will probably discover that you are creating all kinds of shapes. At least three lines must be joined together to create the first rudimentary shape composed of straight lines. The resulting triangle was described by Kandinsky as possessing, *'beginnings and endings which are always present but yielding a constant pressure of movement.'* Other shapes also convey feelings which are determined by the number of sides and degrees of their angles.

As you experiment with curves on your fourth sheet (Fig. 71) and placing them in various directions, you may create waving lines whose undulations seem less agitated than zigzags. However, the extent of their motion depends on the degree of their curvature. If you should allow any of these lines to

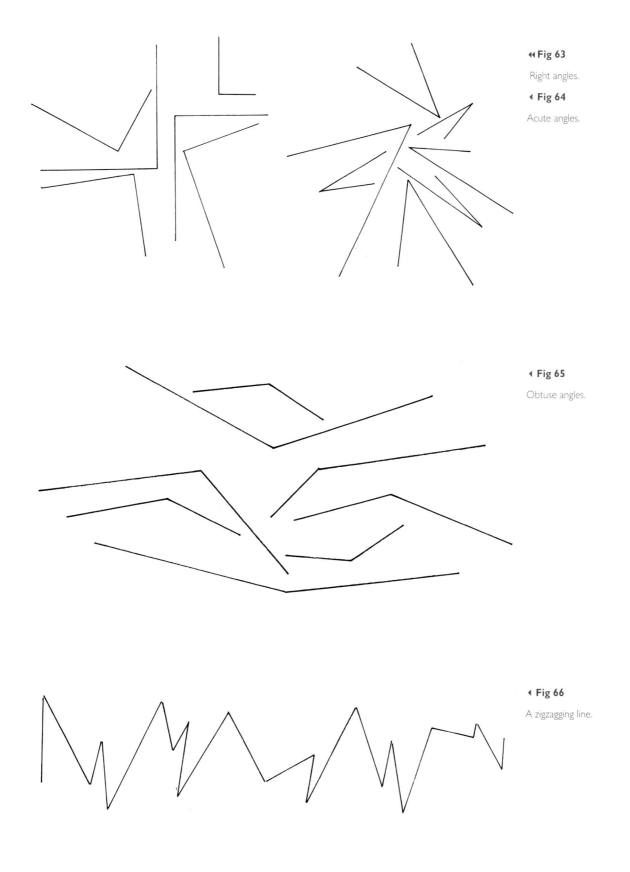

◄ Fig 65

Obtuse angles.

◄ Fig 66

A zigzagging line.

Fig 67 The Peacocks'. Late nineteenth century 'art needlework' silk threads embroidered on silk fabric. From the Margaret Hall-Townley Collection.

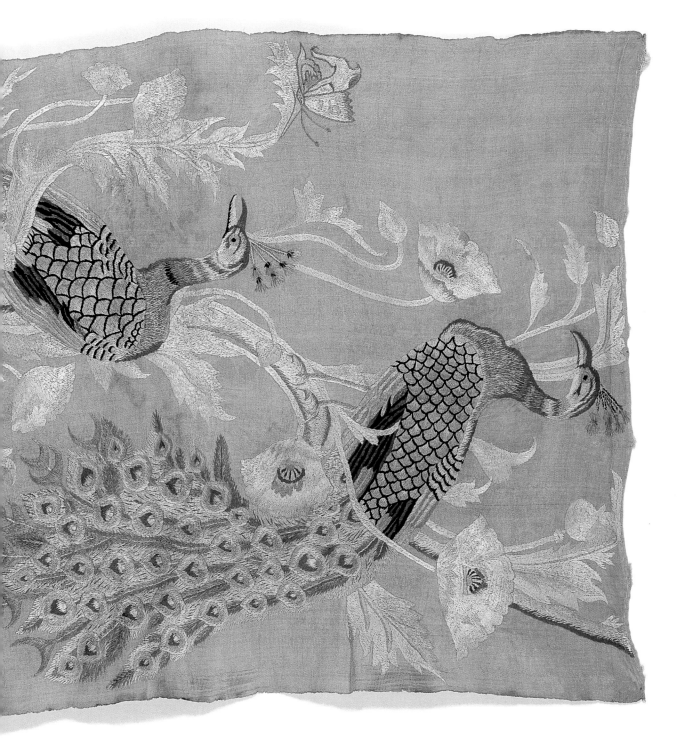

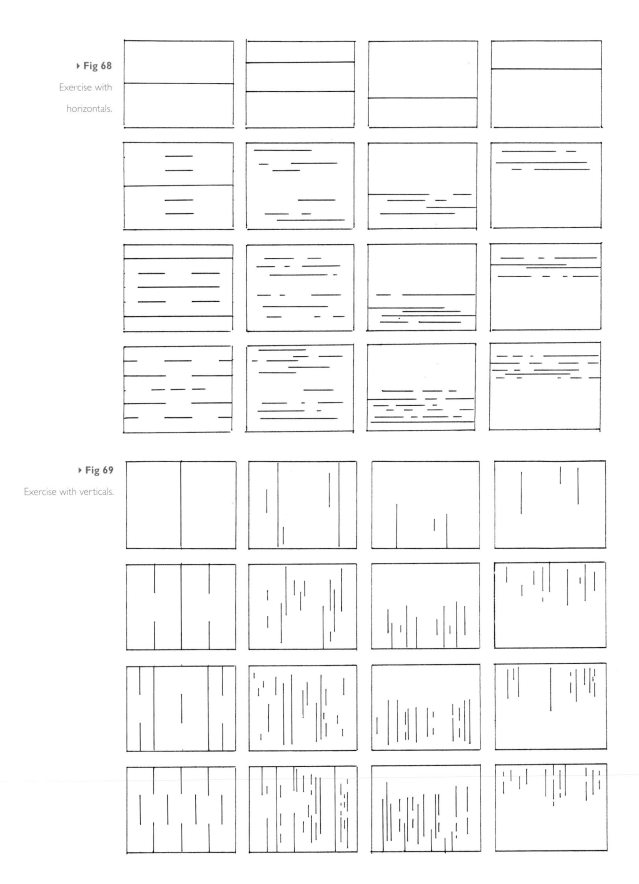

▸ Fig 68

Exercise with
horizontals.

▸ Fig 69

Exercise with verticals.

◄ **Fig 70**

Exercise with obliques.

◄ **Fig 71**

Exercise with curves.

join or overlap each other, you will create curved shapes. Ovals, circles and ellipses are also rudimentary shapes but whose 'beginnings' and 'endings' have disappeared and can express a dynamic repose.

Now complete these four exercises. As always, work in a comfortable position, with speed and rapt attention. Simply perform them contentedly and, for the time being, without judgement so that you can, with freedom from attitude, come to understand and enjoy the nature of all these elements which you are exploring.

Assessment and Evaluation

Strictly speaking this discussion really belongs to Part Four – Design as Process. However, in order to help your present progress, I include it at this stage.

So far I have urged you to refrain from engaging in any kind of criticism of what you do lest it should impede the flow of your creative energies. Criticism is, however, a necessary part of the creative process so long as it is not of an adverse nature based solely on disliking and denigrating what you do. Assessment and evaluation are words with more favourable and positive implications. Assessment is being able to see what has occurred and evaluation is being able to see the value of the occurrence and predicting its appropriate use for the future.

Bearing all this in mind and heart, lay out before you all of the four sheets where you have explored points, lines, directions, angles and shapes. Notice how you have varied their lengths, sizes, amounts and positions. These factors affect the elements themselves and also convey impressions to the mind.

Generally speaking, few elements tend to express quietness, reserve and solitude, whereas many elements tend to express noise, prominence and crowded company. Notice also how the positions of these elements within each rectangle are significant. When placed symmetrically, they seem still; when placed asymmetrically they appear mobile. When placed high, they seem elevated and happy and appear light, free and loose; when placed below they appear heavy, solemn and sad. All such factors are of great significance and purpose to every designer.

Now lay out before you all your previous experiments with colour and texture and engage in the same kind of assessment and evaluation. So far we have been concerned with the nature of each of these elements on their own. Nevertheless, as we have mentioned before, they are all integrated and dependent upon each other. Discussion of specific principles of composition follows very soon in Part Three, for which you can prepare yourself by performing a few more exercises.

Take up a few more sheets on which you have drawn rectangles and draw various combinations of lines, which will result in your creating shapes. Fig. 74 illustrates variations of horizontals combined with verticals. Try this for yourself. Now look back to Fig. 5 illustrating Rosalind Floyd's sample for 'Razzle Dazzle' and you will see that although the composition is based upon a symmetrical balance of verticals and horizontals, all the stitching inclines obliquely. Try another sheet which composes verticals, horizontals and oblique lines together (Fig. 75). Look at Fig. 72, which illustrates an embroidery by Daphne Ashby, and you will see the composition is also based upon a symmetrical balance of the same three types of line but the obliques are given more prominence. Also try combining curves with

◀ **Fig 72** Milanese
Pin Wheel by
Daphne Ashby 1997.
Canvas embroidery
(photograph:
Zul Mukhida).

horizontals and verticals as you can see in Fig. 76. Look at Fig. 73 which is a diagram showing how the design for 'The Buttercup Field' (Fig. 24) is composed mainly of curves inclining towards the horizontal. They represent the undulations of the field and the foliage of the distant trees. The horizontal curves are contrasted by the short vertical lines representing the tree trunks. Try some experiments with all types of lines together as you see in Fig. 77. In fact, try exploring lines and shapes in this way as much as you like. You could even try using colour and texture within some of the designs you create.

Now that you have completed these exercises you are ready to address the next part of the book and enlarge your capacity as a designer by exploring compositional principles.

◀ **Fig 73** Diagram of
curves and verticals in
the design for 'The
Buttercup Field' (fig.24).

71

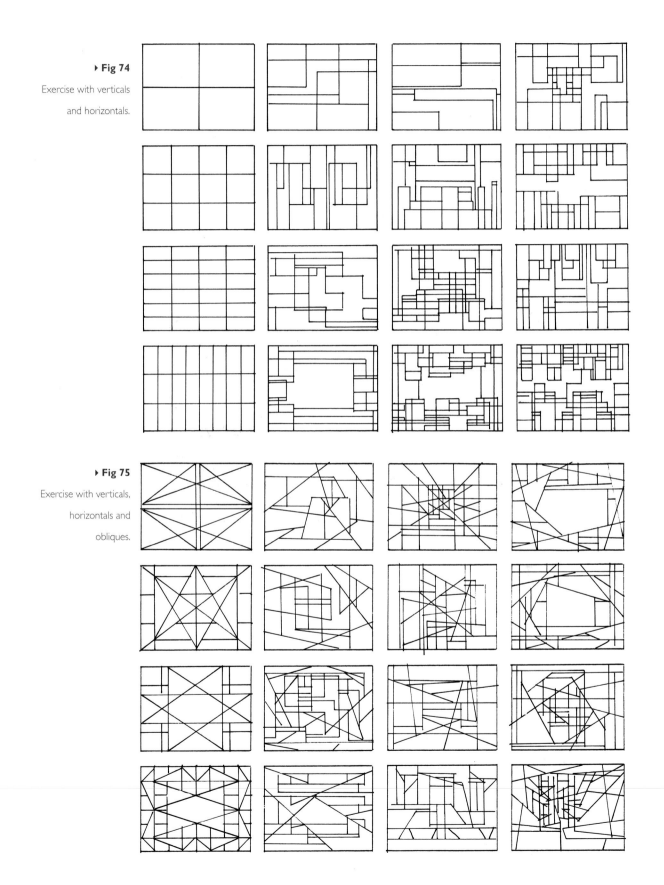

▸ **Fig 74**

Exercise with verticals and horizontals.

▸ **Fig 75**

Exercise with verticals, horizontals and obliques.

◀ **Fig 76**
Exercise with verticals and horizontals and curves.

◀ **Fig 77** Exercise with verticals, horizontals, obliques and curves.

PART THREE

COMPOSITIONAL PRINCIPLES OF DESIGN

'It is not enough that each part has its own particular arrangement and propriety; they must all agree together and make but one harmonious whole.'

Roger de Piles

Composition is the art of fitting together parts to create a unity in the relationship of things with each other. '*Briefly stated*', as Maitland Graves said, '*unity is the cohesion, consistency, oneness and integrity that is the prime essential of composition. Composition implies unity; the words are synonymous.*' This was written fifty years ago, Roger de Piles wrote his statement two hundred and fifty years ago and the following statement was written over two thousand years ago by Aristotle: '*The parts, being so connected that if any of them be either transposed or taken away the whole will be destroyed or changed; for if the presence or absence of something makes no difference it is not a part of the whole.*'.

You will remember reading Kandinsky's statement on composition in the Introduction (p 12), '*The content of a work of art finds its expression in the composition.*' Read now the following statement by Henri Matisse who was writing at about the same time: '*Composition is the art of arranging in a decorative manner the various elements which the artist uses to express his sentiments. In a picture every separate part will be visible and will take up that position, principal or secondary, which suits it best. Everything which has no utility in the picture is for that reason harmful. A work of art implies a harmony of everything together.*' Now that you have read these statements, you will understand that for thousands of years artists and designers all seek a harmonious unity in their compositions. However, it is also important to understand that any rule, device or even principle is governed by one other, overriding, principle of artistic intention. Rules need to be altered for expressive purposes. As John Dewey said '*Rules are part of the game, they are not outside it. No rules: then no game. Different rule: then a different game.*' We shall now explore some rules, devices and principles by which a harmonious unity may be achieved.

'*Art is harmony. Harmony is the analogy of contraries and the analogy of similarities of tone, of colour and of line.*'

George Seurat

impression on the mind and senses, constituting and exhibiting a style.' (René Berger)

'How', you may now well ask, 'is a harmonious and unified composition achieved?' The answer lies in Seurat's statement on this page, where the word 'harmony' is used to mean the fitting together of parts to form a connected whole. Thus we can safely assume that in the visual arts and crafts the word 'harmony' is also synonymous with unity and composition.

In all visual forms of art and craft harmonious and unified compositions arise from a relationship of contrasting and similar elements. Contrast of differences and repetition of similarities are, together, essential agents to their created existence.

Contrast of Differences and Repetition of Similarities

'*Contrast is essential to design. Variety stimulates interest and rouses excitement. Variety vitalises design; spices composition. A composition with too little contrast is monotonous, insipid. Repetition is a basic and common form of natural order. Rhythmic cycles that are eternally repeating the ancient,*

Harmony and Unity

'*Harmony has come to mean a condition in which all the elements of a work combine to produce a unified*

mystical theme of decay and resurrection.'
(Maitland Graves)

Contrast is the life force of design; differences and variations animate, enliven and sometimes excite. Too much contrast causes disruption, anarchy and chaos. Repetition is the pulse of the design's life; similarities regulate, unify and sometimes soothe. Too much repetition can cause monotony, boredom and eventually, like an excess of contrast, conflict. It is as if both qualities meet at their extremities! Thus a certain combination of contrast and repetition are required to create a harmonious unity.

It has been necessary to refer to contrasts of differences and repetition of similarities in Part Two. However we can now discuss them more fully and explore them more expansively. Let us begin by identifying some of them. Refer to Figs 78 to 82 and try tabulating your own experiments.

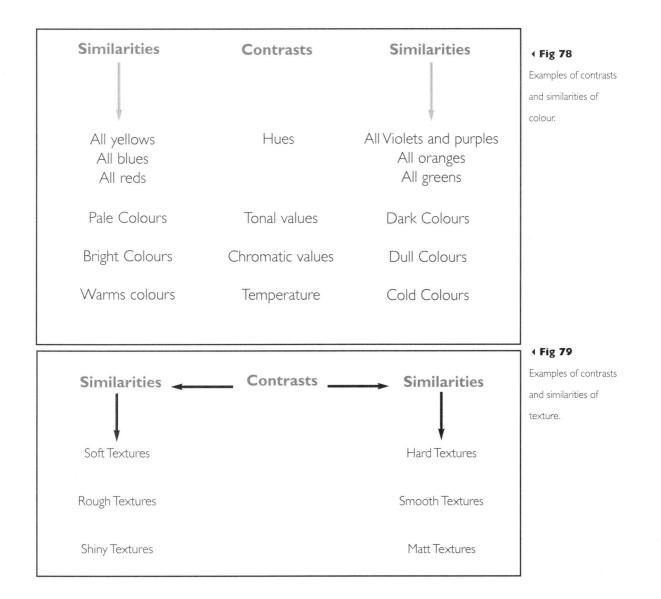

Similarities	Contrasts	Similarities
All yellows All blues All reds	Hues	All Violets and purples All oranges All greens
Pale Colours	Tonal values	Dark Colours
Bright Colours	Chromatic values	Dull Colours
Warms colours	Temperature	Cold Colours

◄ Fig 78

Examples of contrasts and similarities of colour.

Similarities	Contrasts	Similarities
Soft Textures		Hard Textures
Rough Textures		Smooth Textures
Shiny Textures		Matt Textures

◄ Fig 79

Examples of contrasts and similarities of texture.

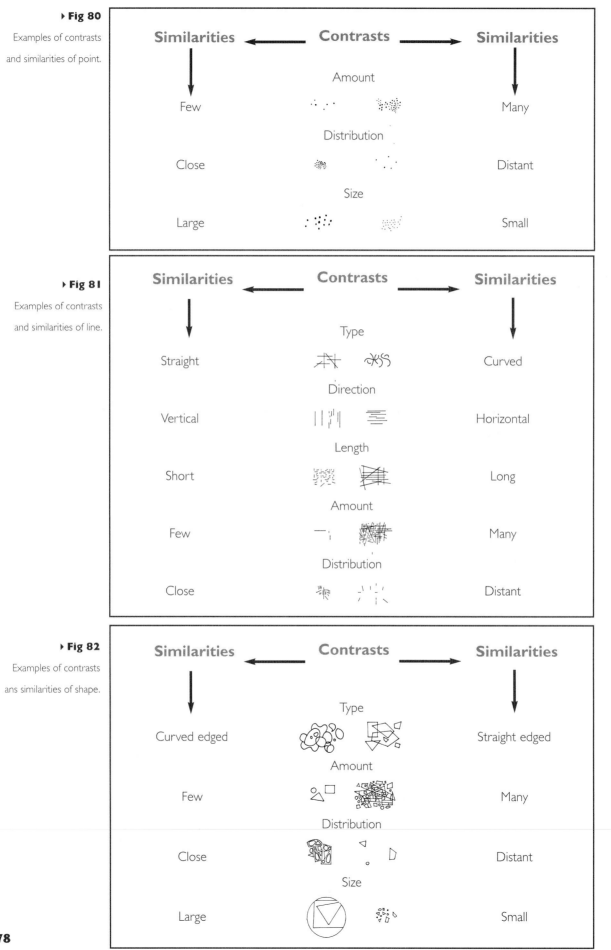

Once you have spent some time tabulating some similarities and contrasts, refer back to some of your previous experiments, particularly those related to Figs 74, 75, 76 and 77, and notice how these were planned so that you not only repeated and contrasted certain elements but also such concomitant factors as sizes, amounts and distribution.

Now that you have supplied yourself with some more factual, rational and objective information, return to the imaginative, spontaneous and intuitive way of working as before and try some more exercises. If you need some more help, read the next two paragraphs first and refer to Figs 83 to 92. However, allow your imagination to be guided rather then dominated by your new knowledge. As Einstein said, 'Imagination is more important than knowledge.'

Fig. 83 illustrates 'Delphiniums'. Figs. 85 to 87 are the diagrams to show you the individual elements of the composition which contribute to integrate the design as a whole (Fig. 84). Fig. 85 shows the distribution and vertical directions, with variously curved inclinations, of the small shapes representing the blue, purple and white flowers. Their sizes both repeat and change. Fig. 86 shows the distribution of the more horizontally distributed shapes representing the orange and yellow flowers. Their sizes are even smaller and there are fewer than their complementary coloured shapes representing the delphiniums. Both are dispersed variously so that some are close together whereas others are further apart. Both are positioned towards the upper part of the picture as a whole to create a feeling of elation. Fig. 87 shows the distribution of slightly curved and oblique lines representing pale green leaves. There are more at the lower part of the design in order to augment the elevation of the flowers which are complemented also by the dispersal of these curved and oblique lines in horizontal strips. All shapes and lines are placed over a large area of very dark green representing the distance. This dark tonal value contrasts, manifests and enlivens all the other elements which, you can understand, are variously repeated and contrasted in some way in order to achieve a harmonious unity to the composition.

Similar principles were applied to the composition of 'Cornflowers and Marigolds' (Fig. 88). Fig. 89 shows how it has been composed with lines in many directions. Fig. 90 shows the distribution of a star-burst arrangement of lines to represent the marigolds and Fig. 91

'Of course the character of everything is best manifested by contrast. Rest can only be enjoyed after labour; sound, to be heard clearly, must arise out of silence; light is exhibited by darkness, darkness by light; and so on in all doings.'

John Ruskin

▶ **83** 'Delphiniums' by the author 1998. Fabric collage with machine and hand embroidery.

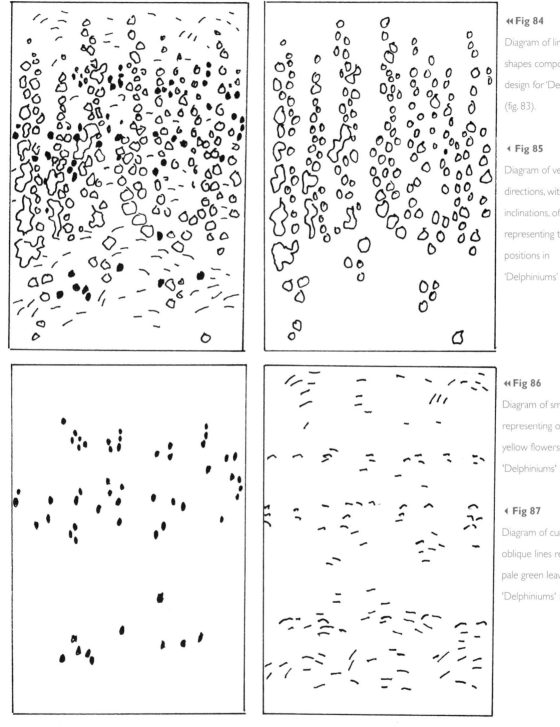

◀◀ **Fig 84**

Diagram of lines and shapes composing the design for 'Delphiniums' (fig. 83).

◀ **Fig 85**

Diagram of vertical directions, with curved inclinations, of shapes representing the flower positions in 'Delphiniums' (fig. 83).

◀◀ **Fig 86**

Diagram of small shapes representing orange and yellow flowers in 'Delphiniums' (fig.83).

◀ **Fig 87**

Diagram of curved and oblique lines representing pale green leaves in 'Delphiniums' (fig 83).

▶ **Fig 88** 'Cornflowers and Marigolds' by the author 1998. Fabric collage with machine and hand embroidery.

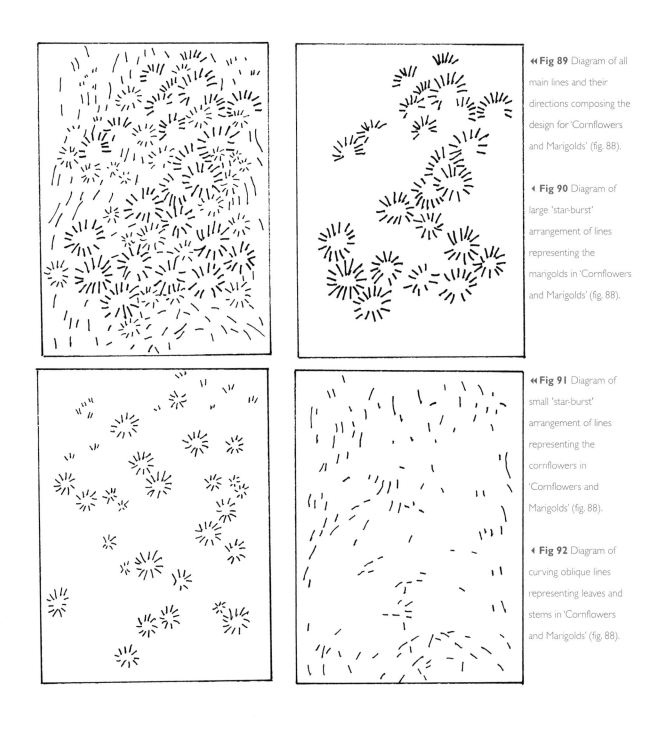

Fig 89 Diagram of all main lines and their directions composing the design for 'Cornflowers and Marigolds' (fig. 88).

Fig 90 Diagram of large 'star-burst' arrangement of lines representing the marigolds in 'Cornflowers and Marigolds' (fig. 88).

Fig 91 Diagram of small 'star-burst' arrangement of lines representing the cornflowers in 'Cornflowers and Marigolds' (fig. 88).

Fig 92 Diagram of curving oblique lines representing leaves and stems in 'Cornflowers and Marigolds' (fig. 88).

shows the same for the smaller cornflowers. Their sizes, respectively, repeat and change and whereas the generally larger marigolds are disposed close together, the smaller cornflowers are dispersed further apart. Complementary colours, tonal values and chromatic values are similarly repeated and contrasted. Fig. 92 shows the distribution of curving oblique lines representing leaves and stems placed throughout the design. Many tend to curve downwards at the lower part and soar upwards towards the top. However, some counterchange is employed to prevent the design being split in two halves. Once again all elements are variously repeated and contrasted in order to achieve an integrity to the composition.

When you perform your exercises, try some using similar and contrasting tones and colours as well as points, lines and shapes. Explore texture in the same way so that you bring together as many of the formal elements as you can. As I said earlier, perform these exercises spontaneously and intuitively so that the natural rhythms of your innate designing capacity allow themselves to take full control. Reminded by the Duke Ellington statement, *'It don't mean a thing, if it ain't got that swing,'* I attmpted to create the alternating movements of the honeysuckle flowers and stems so that they swing in the breeze as they do in their natural environment (Figs 93 and 94). This leads us on to explore our next principles of composition:

◄◄Fig 93 Honeysuckle, 1998 by the author. Fabric collage with machine and hand embroidery.

rhythm and alternation. You will notice that these principles and all those for discussion and exploration in this part of the book are based upon the relationship between repetition of similarities and contrasts of differences.

Rhythm and Alternation

Rhythms and alternating sequences are part of our very existence as evinced by the regularity of every heartbeat and the inhaling and exhaling of our breathing. It is no surprise that we need to show such rhythms in our artistic expressions. Music and poetry depend upon them. So do the visual art forms; particularly decorative designs. Look now at Fig. 97 which illustrates a collection of late nineteenth and early twentieth-century braids, and also at Fig. 98 which illustrates the alternating sequences of their construction. Try some experiments yourself and, as before, include tone, colour and texture as part of your schemes.

Fig. 101 illustrates a detail of a mid nineteen-twenties evening coat which involves a subtle system of rhythmic alternations where similar motifs never quite repeat themselves exactly. Look carefully at the illustration and at the diagrams (Figs 95 and 96) to see how the dynamic design is composed of circles, half-

'Alternation is a succession of two objects recurring regularly in turn; and the cadence of appearance and disappearance gives pleasure to the success.'

Lady Marion M. Alford

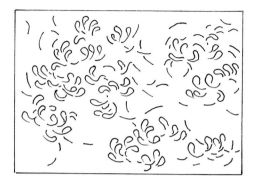

Figure and Ground

I wonder whether you have ever questioned the term 'negative spaces' because of the inferiority of its implication. Although we must avoid becoming embroiled with semantics, it is worth stressing again how every part of a design has its own relative significance.

The alternation between figure and ground is often discussed in the relatively recent studies in the psychology of human perception. However, the phenomenon has shown itself since early times. Many architectural features are based upon alternating rhythms where every feature is positive. For examples, the rolling sequence of the Greek Scroll (Fig. 99) and the more severe continuity of the Key Pattern (Fig. 100) awaken in us the knowledge that

circles and fan shapes linked by intricate embroidery and highlighted by various styles, sizes and shapes of beads. Irene Barnes, in whose collection this garment can be found displayed at the Manor House Museum in Bury St. Edmonds, writes, '*Many hours of work have gone into adorning the evening coat of cream coloured satin onto which is set a dynamic design of circles cut by interlacing half-circles and fan shapes. Black satin fans intermingle with hand-printed pink and darker pink fans and semi-circles. A combination of Cornely embroidery, beads, appliqué and printing all make this costume totally unique.*'

'We are forced to recognise the fact that in the field of vision nothing is negative; the space round and in the image is as positive as the image itself.'

Maurice de Sausmarez.

all parts of the designs are important. You will notice in the diagrams (Fig. 99 b. and c. and Fig. 100 b. and c.)

◀ Fig 94 Diagram of curved lines and their various directions composing the design for 'Honeysuckle.' (Fig. 93)

◀ Figs 95 and 96 Diagrams of alternating patterns comprising the design for 'Evening Coat' (Fig 101). (Author's copies from originals by Irene Barnes.)

▶ **Fig 97** Embroidered Braids (private collection)

(a) Edwardian Schiffli machine-embroidered. Satin stitch with silk floss and metallic gold on satin ribbon.

(b) 1930s Schiffli machine-embroidered with silk floss on cotton net.

(c) 1920s Pantograph Schiffli machine-embroidered with silk floss on cotton lawn. Ribbons are intended to be threaded through the slots.

(d) Edwardian Beaded and gold tambour work on black silk net with gold cord.

(e) 1930s East European. Hand-embroidered silk floss on linen.

(f) Edwardian Machine-embroidered metallic thread on cotton net. Flowers are padded by their shapes being previously embroidered with cotton threads.

(g) Early Twentieth Century Passementerie in the Spanish style. Constructed with the needle from already-formed braids and sequins.

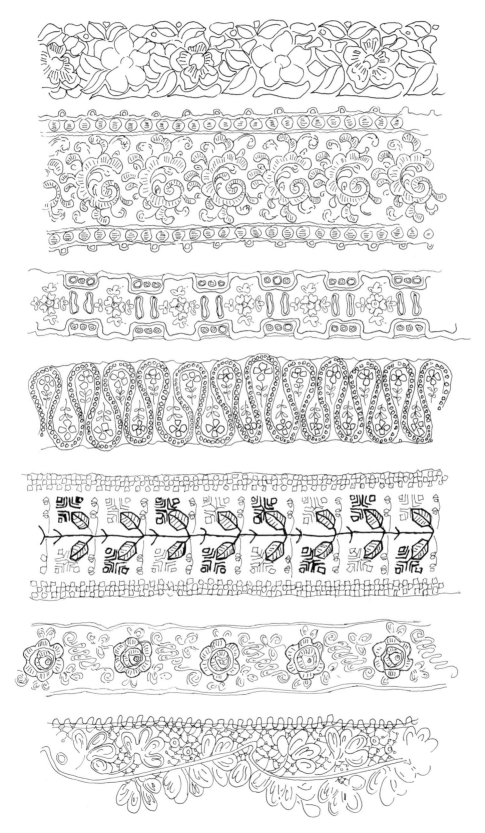

◀ **Fig 98** Diagrams of
alternating sequences for
fig.99: (a), (b), (c), (d), (e),
(f), and (g).

a

◀ **Fig 99**
Alternating rhythms
between 'figure' and
'ground' in Greek Scroll
pattern (a), (b), and (c).

b

c

◀ **Fig 100**
Alternating rhythms
between 'figure' and
'ground' in Greek Key
pattern (a), (b), and (c).

a

b

◀◀ **Fig 101** Evening coat,
mid 1920s. Combined
techniques of Cornely
embroidery, beading,
appliqué and printing.
From the Irene Barnes
Collection at the Manor
House Museum, Bury St.
Edmunds. (Photograph :
Tony Kora.).

c

▶ **Fig 102(a)**

Diagram of lines composing the wallpaper design, 'Poppies and Peacocks.' Late nineteenth century. Influenced by the Arts and Crafts Movement.

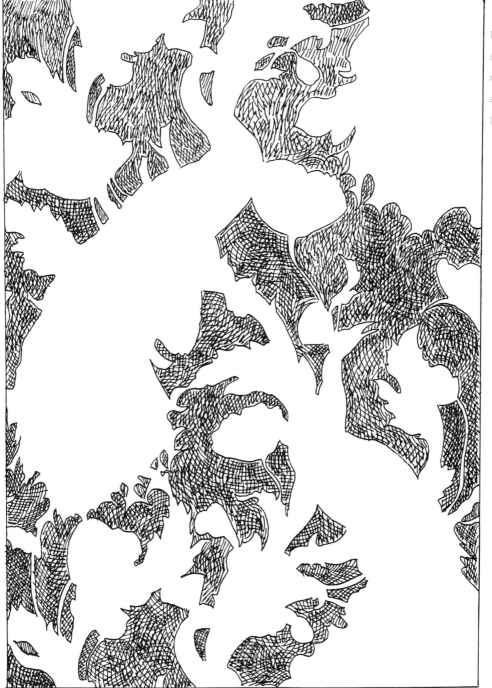

◀ **Fig 102 (b)**

Diagram indicating the
shapes in between the
main motifs of 'Poppies
and Peacocks.'
(Fig 102(a))

that at one moment the black emerges from the white and at another moment the white emerges from the black.

Dominance and Subordinance

Most designers intend to resolve such prevarications caused by equality between figure and ground by employing the principle of dominance and subordinance. You will notice that all the other illustrations in this book employ this principle and so also does the design of the wallpaper depicting 'Peacocks and Poppies' illustrated in Fig. 102 (a. and b.), which, incidentally, you may notice is derived from the same source as the embroidery illustrated in Fig. 67. If you look at Fig. 102 (a.) you will see that the dominant areas are the peacocks and poppies and if you look at Fig. 102 (b.) that the subsidiary areas are those in between them. However, notice also that these subsidiary areas have their own positive importance as well as assisting those which are dominant.

A useful exercise is to trace a design which you admire and trace the shapes in between those which are dominant so that you consolidate your

understanding of what Alexander Pope said: 'All are but parts of one stupendous whole ' and, as you read earlier, 'The space round and in the image is as positive as the image itself .' This method is also a useful way of assessing how all parts of the designs, which we ourselves create, are integrated and unified. Try some and see!

Gradation, Progression and Radiation

Gradation and progression imply change and movement which are essential to life itself. Therefore they are valuable and useful devices for artistic expression.

All scales are forms of progression and gradation. The word 'scale' derives from the Latin word *scala* which means steps. *Scala* itself probably had its origins in the Sanskrit word *skand* which means to ascend. You have already explored some form of scales with hue, tone and chromatic values in Part Two of this book. Indeed, because you have allowed your natural designing capacity to flow intuitively, you may have created scales with some of the other elements instinctively. Look back at some of your

'Gradation is a common and basic form of natural order.
It exists in the ascending crescendo of sunrise and in the falling diminuendo of twilight silently blending into darkness.'

Maitland Graves

exercises with point, line direction and shape to see whether this is so.

Make some diagrams like those you see in Fig. 103 so that you create a progression between points and lines by grading their sizes, lengths or direction. Notice how this principle allows the contrast of differences to be reconciled by similar steps.

Now look at the cashmere shawl (Fig. 104), which is embroidered with various motifs including the 'buta' and the 'mandala', and notice how they are linked by other gradual patterns within the motifs and throughout the entire design itself. Look also at the tent stitched rug (Fig. 105) and notice how contrasting motifs and colours are linked by graded steps of line and tone.

Radiation is one of the most basic principles of gradation of natural order. It occurs in spiders' webs, snowflakes and many flowers. Look back at the 'Jackmanii *Clematis*' (Fig. 33) and ahead to the illustrations depicting a spider's web (Fig. 115) and a hawthorn tree (Figs 116 and 117) to see how graduation of direction can be employed to create aesthetic designs.

Try some exercises and employ the principles of gradation, progression and radiation yourself.

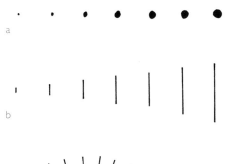

a

b

c

d

e

◄ **Fig 103**

Diagram of various forms of gradation, progression and radiation:
(a) Gradation of size of points. (b) Gradation of length of lines. (c) Gradation of direction of lines (d) Gradation of types, lengths and direction of lines. (e) Radiation of lines and shapes from central point.

Geometry, Mathematics and Proportion

Did you find the abstract concepts of geometry and mathematics difficult at school to the point of loathing the subjects? If so, take care not to skip these pages! You may discover that you will change your attitude completely. It was, indeed, through embroidery that I discovered that these disciplines were not only essential to all visual forms of art and craft but became exciting and enjoyable when they became relevant by means of practical application; I could play creative games with measurement and proportion to some purpose. So try a few exercises yourself as if you were playing games.

Let us start with symmetry. Strictly speaking symmetry is the exact juxtaposition of equal parts in correspondence with each other. The embroidered purse (Fig. 107) is a fine example of

▶▶**Fig 104**

Cashmere shawl. c1840. Hand-embroidered in stem stitch. The 'buta' and the 'mandala' are symbolic of growth and eternity. The continuity of the patterns reflects the order of the universe. From the Margaret Hall-Townley Collection.

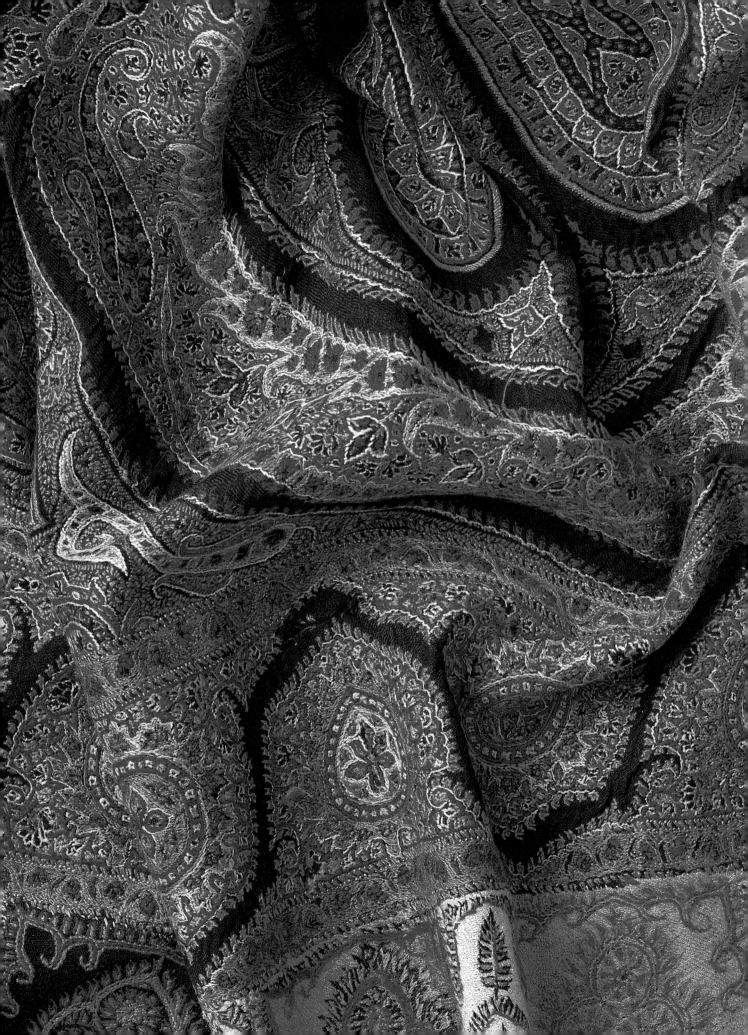

symmetry and so are Rosalind Floyd's and Daphne Ashby's designs (Figs 5 and 72). Look back to Figs 68 to 71, and 74 to 77, and notice how the first columns on the left of all the designs are symmetrical. Try some further exercises like these and use colour and texture correspondingly.

'If arithmetic, measurement and weighting be taken out of any art, that which remains will not be much.'

Plato

outward form are exactly the same; thus we also need to express variation. The Royal Coat of Arms (Fig. 106) is a splendidly embroidered example of variation within a symmetrical balance. Try some exercises now which include variations within your symmetrical balancing acts.

« Fig 105

Embroidered rug by Robin Giddings 1991 to 1992. Half-cross stitch canvas work in tapestry wools.

We are all born with a sense of symmetry to match our outward form; we appreciate its existence and instinctively feel the need to express it in our designs. However, no two sides of our

Asymmetrical designs also need to balance so that a harmonious relationship is achieved among the elements. 'How', you may ask, 'is this achieved?' The answer lies in the concept of geometric

‹ Fig 106

Royal Coat of Arms by staff and apprentices of the Royal School of Needlework 1994. Silk and gold threads on silk and velvet fabric. From the Royal School of Needlework collection. (Photograph: RSN.)

proportion. Try this exercise to discover the most popular balance between two unequal parts. Draw a straight line of any length. Let us choose one of eight units. Now divide it into two unequal parts so as to create a harmonious and aesthetically satisfying relationship between them. There is, and always has been, an instinctive tendency to divide the line approximately into one third and two thirds rather than one eighth and seven eighths. Look at Fig. 108 which illustrates the average and intuitive preference.

There is also a way by which an ideal relationship between these two parts can be achieved rationally by deliberate geometric calculation. Discover this way yourself by copying the diagram in Fig. 109 and following the instructions in the caption.

When you have completed this exercise, you will see that you have not only made the ideal division between the two lines B F and C E at points A and D respectively but also created two ideal rectangles B C E F and A D E F whose proportions are exactly the same. This proportion was first described as the 'Golden Ratio' by Euclid, the father of all geometry, in about 300 BC; Renaissance artists, philosophers and architects called it the 'Divine Proportion', and since the nineteenth century it has been known as the 'Golden Section'.

◄◄ Fig 107 'Gold Work Purse' by Amanda Ewing 1998. Gold, silver and coloured threads embroidered into manipulated metallic tissue by various techniques including *Or Nué*. From the Royal School of Needlework Collection.

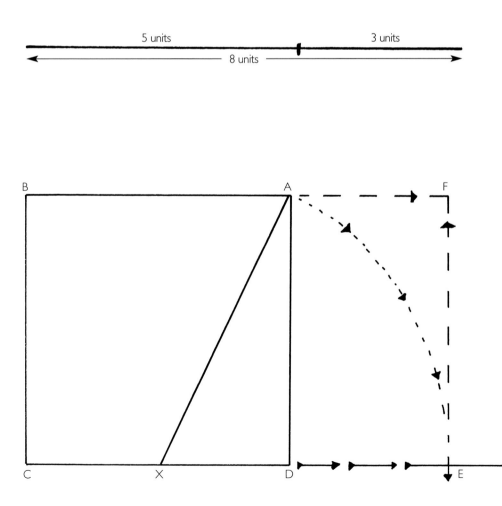

◄ Fig 108
The average and intuitive preference of dividing a line into two unequal parts.

◄ Fig 109
The geometric calculation of the Golden Section. Draw a square A B C D. Halve it at C D exactly and mark it X. Place the point of a pair of compasses at X with the pencil point at A to create a radius and describe an arc downwards. Extend C D to meet the arc at E. Extend B A and draw a perpendicular line upwards from E so they meet at point F.

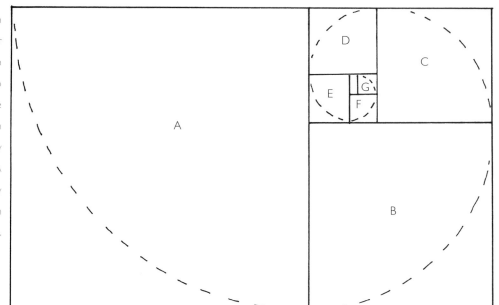

▶ **Fig 110** Formation of a spiral. Draw another Golden Rectangle (as in fig. 109) and continue to subtract successive squares (A to G) from each subsequently smaller rectangle. A spiral can be formed by drawing arcs in each square.

▶ **Fig 110** Formation of a spiral. Draw another Golden Rectangle (as in fig. 109) and continue to subtract successive squares (A to G) from each subsequently smaller rectangle. A spiral can be formed by drawing arcs in each square.

▶ **Fig 111** In a pentagon there is a Golden Section relationship between any diagonal and any of its sides, and also in the way the diagonals intersect each other. Thus A C : A B, A D : D C and A E : E D are all the same ratio.

There are many other games you can play with geometry. Try just two more. Figs 110 and 111 show how a spiral and a pentagon, respectively, are formed by the principle of the Golden Section.

Apparently the only way to produce this ratio exactly is by geometric rather than mathematical means which can only approximate it. Nevertheless, a medieval scholar called Fibonacci discovered an intriguing sequence of numbers which is formed by each one being the sum of the two which precede it (Fig. 112). The higher the numbers (e.g. 89 = 144) the closer the ratio is to the Golden Section.

Such geometric proportions and mathematical ratios govern the structure of plant and animal life, manifesting themselves in shells, seed pods and cell growth. Fibonacci himself first discovered his famous sequence by calculating the rate of propagation from a pair of rabbits. The most notable examples of this natural design are the pine cone and the chrysanthemum. Look at the diagram for the former

(Fig. 113) and you can count five spirals arranged in one direction and eight in the other. Now look at the diagram for the latter (Fig. 114) and you will see how the spirals are arranged in sets of twenty-one and thirty-four.

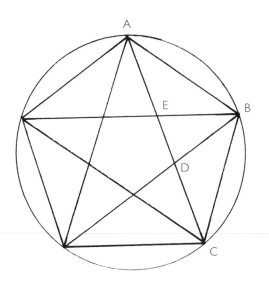

1, 1, 2, 3, 5, 8, 13, 21, 34, 55, 89, 144

◄ **Fig 112**

The Fibonacci Series.

The principle of the Golden Section is used by all artists and designers to a certain extent , either intuitively, by spontaneous approximation or rationally, by geometric or mathematical calculation. It is important to remember that any device is governed by artistic and expressive intention. If you look at most illustrations in this book, you will detect that certain elements have been arranged in such a way. Let us look at just three examples. In Fig. 1, which illustrates a pin cushion, you will see a symmetrical balance of shapes, colours and textures within a square format. However, you will also see that the amount of blue is approximately one third of the whole compared with the two thirds of its complementary colour, orange. In Fig. 31 the same pair of complementary colours are used in the same proportion but their roles are reversed. Notice

how the sea-horse, which is the main feature of the mirror's cover, is placed one third towards the upper part of the design.

Finally, look at Fig. 115, which illustrates 'The Blackberries and the Spider's Web'. The web itself, as in nature, is formed by a spiral on radials and is placed one third towards the upper left part of the design. There is only one web, two other subsidiary features (flowers and blackberries), three flowers, five blackberries composed in silver fabric, eight blackberries in shiny fabric and thirteen unbroken radials in the spider's web and thirteen obvious blackberries. However, if you look carefully you can detect two broken radials and two more and somewhat disguised blackberries. The 'rule' has been deliberately broken to match the non-conformity in Nature where many anomalies can be found.

◄◄ **Fig 113** Diagram of the double spiral formation of the fir cone arranged in sets of five and nine.

◄ **Fig 114** Diagram of the double spiral formation of the fir cone arranged in sets of twenty one and thirty four.

« **Fig 115**

'Blackberries and the Spider's Web' by the author 1996. Fabric collage with machine embroidery.

Complexity and Simplicity

To follow the complex patterns in Byzantine mosaics, Celtic manuscripts or Gothic traceries creates excitement, curiosity and discovery. Lady Marion Alford writes, '*It gives the mind the pleasure of untying the Gordian Knot without cutting it.*' We have already observed some of the many complex patterns in Nature on the preceding pages. To these we can add the microcosmic structure of snowflakes or the formation of crystals to the macrocosmic design of the universe itself. Common to all is the simplicity of design as a whole and the immediacy of its impact. This

synthesis was described by Paul Gauguin as, '*Complication of the idea through simplification of the form.*' Look back at some of the illustrations and notice how those which contain intricate patterns are integrated by simple forms. For example, thousands of little shapes which decorate the Sindhi wedding dress (Fig. 40) are bound by simple horizontal and vertical directions. Another example is how the simple horizontal format of the rag rug (Fig. 52) holds in equilibrium the complex array of colours dispersed in a myriad of permutations.

Now look at Figs 116 and 117 which illustrates 'The Irish believe that the Hawthorn belongs to the Faeries.' Here again we can comprehend one single and simple image which, at the same time, is composed of wonderful, intricate and complex patterns. Margaret Hall-Townley created this

'Simplicity is not an end in art, but one arrives at simplicity in

spite of oneself, in approaching the real sense of things.

Simplicity is complexity itself and one has to be nourished by its

essence in order to understand its value.'

Constantin Brancusi.

stunning embroidery using solid straight stitches on a domestic sewing machine. Although she does not believe in the post-Shakespearean concept of fairies she says 'I do believe in Nature Energies, I am fascinated by the tradition of the hawthorn tree belonging to the Earth Goddess. It is a fundamental part of our rural environment which is crucial to our survival. I am concerned that the countryside is vanishing. We should slow down and realise how important is Nature and all of her mysteries before it is all scooped up by machines. The embroidery is to be seen in two ways; once with normal lighting from the front (Fig. 116) and again with light shining from behind (Fig. 117). Imagine going for a walk in the woods on a grey Autumn day; you look up at a Hawthorn tree and it may seem dull and gloomy. Then, suddenly the sun comes out, all the berries are ablaze with colour and you feel really uplifted!'

Now try some exercises where you integrate complexity with simplicity. As you journey towards the close of this part of the book, allow your imagination to create harmony from confusion with all the elements at your disposal by employing the principles, laws, rules, systems and devices about which you have been reading and exploring. At certain times, with a cool head and a warm heart, assess and evaluate what you have done. Remember to correct, change and develop in a positive manner so that your voyage of discovery is not impeded by dread, doubt and denigration. Now we shall move to the last part of this book and investigate how our very thought processes govern the way we design.

'The artist is born to pick and choose, and group with science

these elements, that the result may be beautiful - as the musi-

cian gathers his notes and forms from his chords until he bring

forth from chaos glorious harmony.'

James A. McNeil Whistler.

▶▶Fig 116

'The Irish Believe that the Hawthorn belongs to the Faeries' 1996. Machine embroidery. Margaret Hall-Townley (lit from the front).

▶▶Fig 117

(lit from the back).

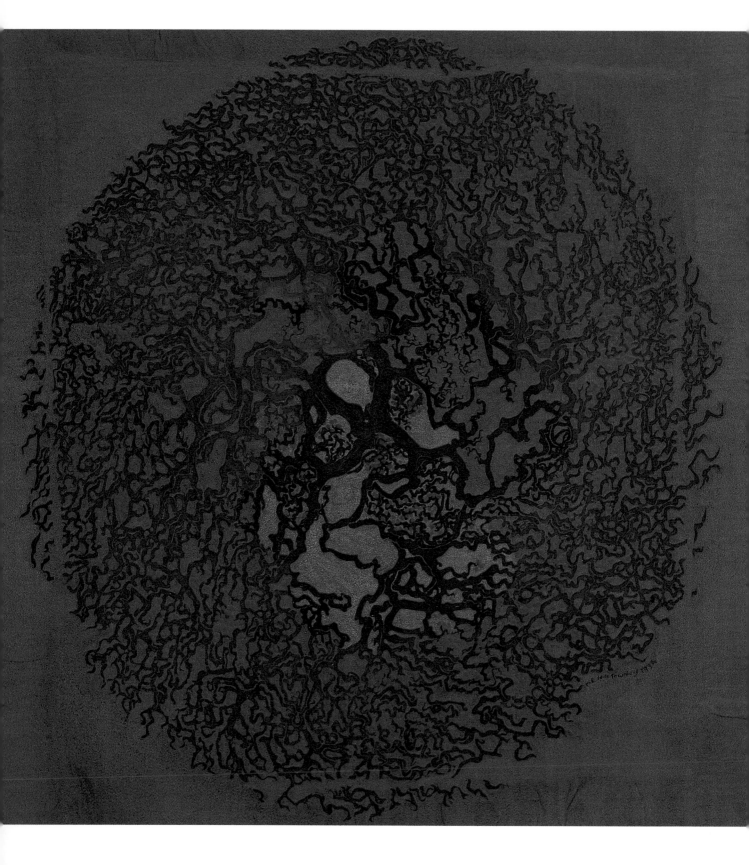

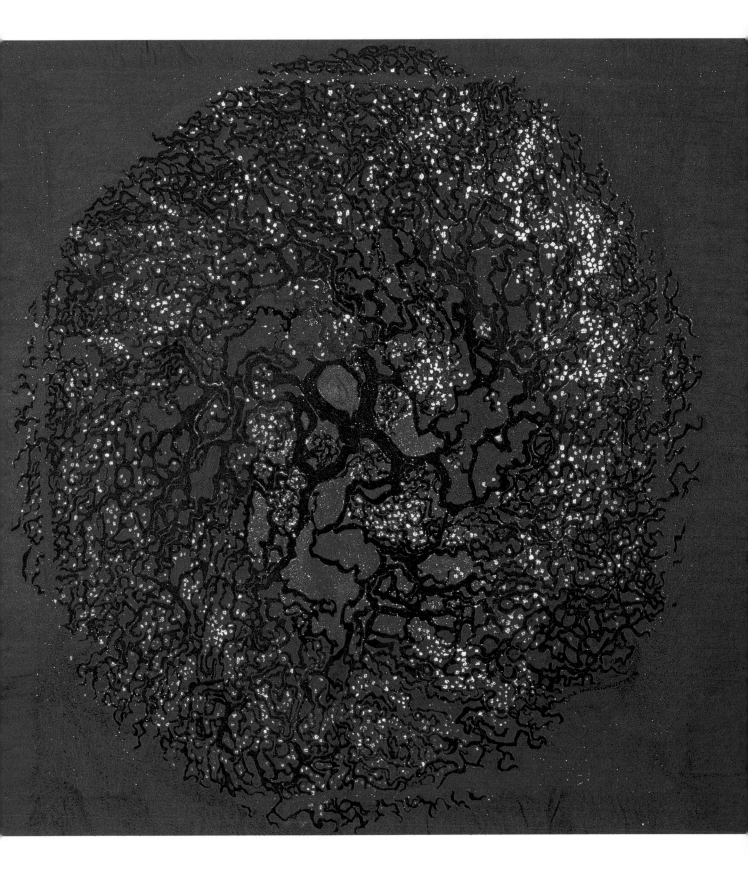

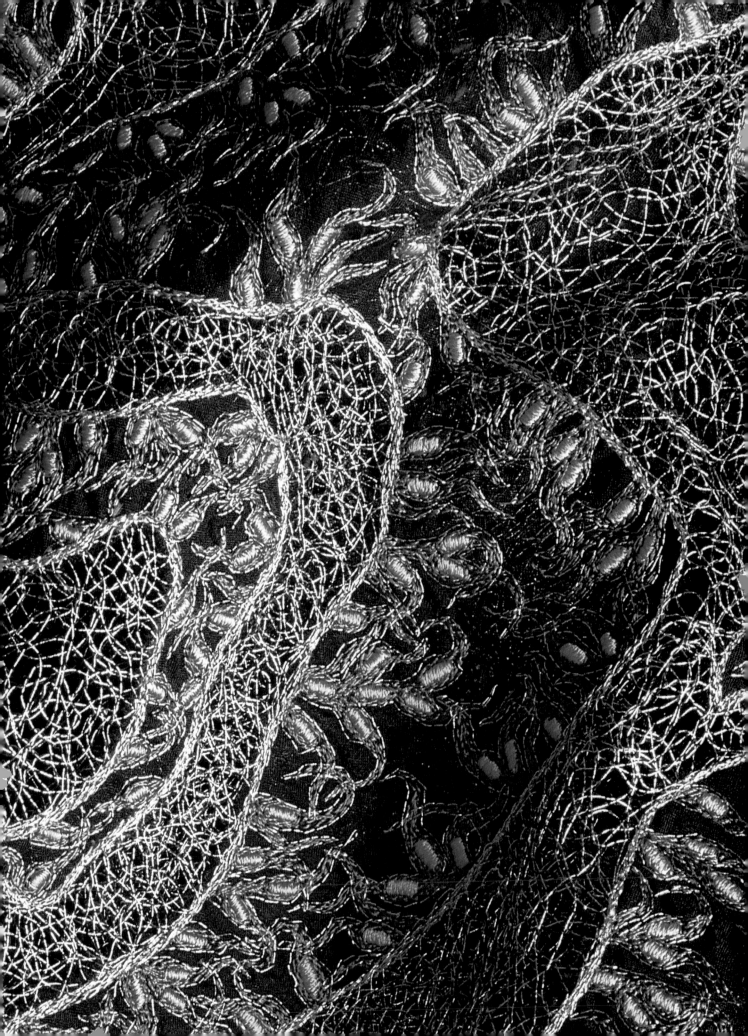

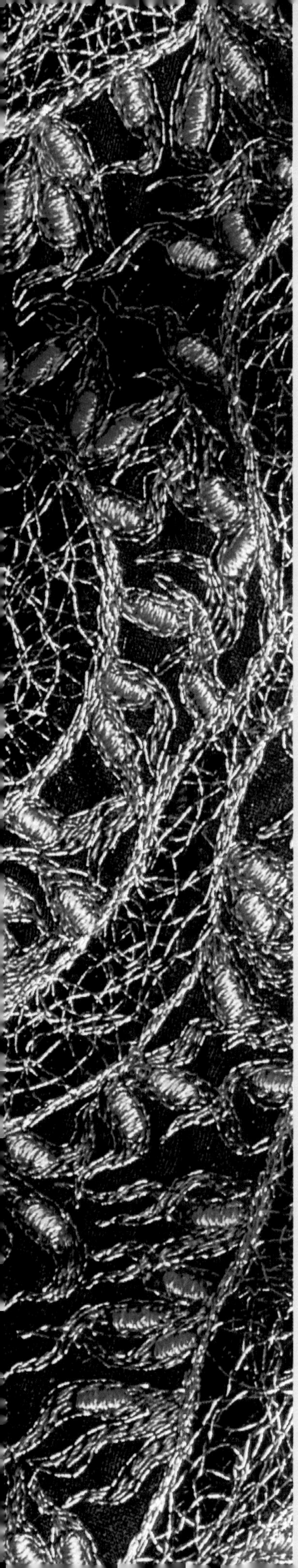

PART FOUR

THE CREATIVE
PROCESS OF
DESIGN

'Now, you of noble mind who

are about to join this profession,

begin by decking yourselves

with this attire: love, enthusiasm,

reverence, obedience and constancy.'

Cennino Cennini

Writing his book on art - *Il Libro dell' Arte* - in about 1390 Cennino
Cennini begins with this exhortation to us his readers by addressing
the attitudes of our minds that promote creative thinking.
Fundamentally all creativity is based upon creative *thinking*.
Furthermore, the potential to be creative is inherent in all of us,
otherwise we would not be human; it distinguishes us from all other
forms of life. On the whole we tend to assume that only a few
people are born creative and the rest of us muddle through life as
best we can. It is more to the point to say that there is little scope in

our cultural systems for us to develop our potential to be and behave creatively.

Fortunately, during the past few decades, enough research has been done to prove that if a more favourable climate were provided, we could all behave as creative individuals. Firstly, we need to foster certain attitudes which Cennino Cennini mentioned so long ago. Love, enthusiasm and respect for what we do are clearly essential. The old maxim, 'Where there is a will there is a way', is an endorsement. It helps if others around us hold the same attitudes; encouragement from without promotes motivation from within. Seeds grow in good soil as the 'Parable of the Sower' explains. Obedience to rules is somewhat necessary. It has been said that rules need to be broken. However, you can only break things if you hold or have some connection with them. Furthermore, it is important not to confuse rules with laws, and laws with principles. You have experienced this distinction earlier and we shall discuss it further under the heading, 'Flexibility'. Finally, we need to foster constancy. It is a teacher's role to encourage. So far I have tried to encourage your love, enthusiasm and respect for what you do and withheld the fact that anything worth doing well can be arduous and uncertain. We shall discuss how we must persevere with our efforts under the heading, 'Fluency.'

Creativity is a precious gift and needs to be nurtured with care. The degree to which we allow this innate capacity to develop and flourish determines the quality of what we do and how we

'No creative work is possible unless it is based on a sensitive experience.'

Viktor Lowenfeld

do it. Therefore, as designers and embroiderers we need to employ all the powers of our creativity at our disposal. Let us now investigate the individual characteristics of our creative capacities.

Sensitivity

Theories of perception, particularly those proposed by the Gestalt psychologists, have shown that we are inclined to develop habits of seeing what we want or expect to see. Curiosity and interest need to be constantly involved in order for us to react beyond stereotyped responses and move towards a greater awareness. Attention is also necessary. However, attention needs to be relaxed as Robert McKim said: '*By relaxing irrelevant tension, the individual releases full energy and attention to the task in hand.*' At the start of Part Two of this book you will recall that I suggested meditating for a while just before working. A useful form of meditation is quietly and deliberately being aware of each of our five senses, which we normally take for granted, in order to realise their full importance. As Jean-Jacques Rousseau said: '*Everything that comes to the mind enters through the gate of sense.*' It also trains our minds to be in the present and free from irrelevant thoughts. We recognise past knowledge and future intentions are important. However, they can only be experienced by our being sensitive to the present time. According to A.N. Whitehead, '*The understanding of what we* want is an understanding of an insistent present. The only use of a knowledge from the past is to equip us for the present. The present contains all that there is, it is holy ground; for it is the past and it is the future.'

The sense of touch is very important to all textile artists. Indeed it was the sumptuous variety of textures in fabric and thread that attracted me to take up embroidery in the first place. We need to understand the nature of the materials we use, learn what they are like and what they like to do. This is achieved primarily through the sense of touch. I was amused but more delighted to hear a reply to a question from one person to another at a craft fair: '*What are you going to do with all those?*' said one, pointing to a large packet of fabric pieces which the other had just purchased. Swiftly came the answer, '*I'm going to take them home and stroke them!*'

Sight is also very important and drawing helps us to see. However, when I mention the word 'Drawing' to groups or individual embroiderers the usual response is, '*I'm terrified of drawing!*' It was this reaction which prompted me to call my

drawing courses for the last thirty years and a recently published book, *Drawing for the Terrified.*

Although it is not essential to be able to draw in order to design abstract compositions or embroider them, it is of a huge benefit if naturalistic and descriptive elements are involved. More importantly, drawing is a discipline which is primarily concerned with developing our sensitive awareness. The terrors we experience are mainly of the unknown and failure. Terror of the unknown can be dispelled by learning to draw with a good teacher; I highly recommend *Drawing on the Right Side of the Brain* by Betty Edwards. Terror of failure can be dispelled by focusing on seeing and the actual process of drawing so that the attention is distracted from speculation. Drawing, under the guidance of Betty Edwards, will also help you to develop the spatial, holistic and intuitive faculties that are located in the right hemisphere of the brain and which are complementary to the logical, analytical and rational faculties which reside on the

'*Drawing is a means of finding your way about things, and a way of experiencing more quickly, certain tryouts and attempts.*'

Henry Moore

'*I would rather teach drawing that my pupils may learn to love nature, than to teach the looking at nature that they may learn to draw.*'

John Ruskin

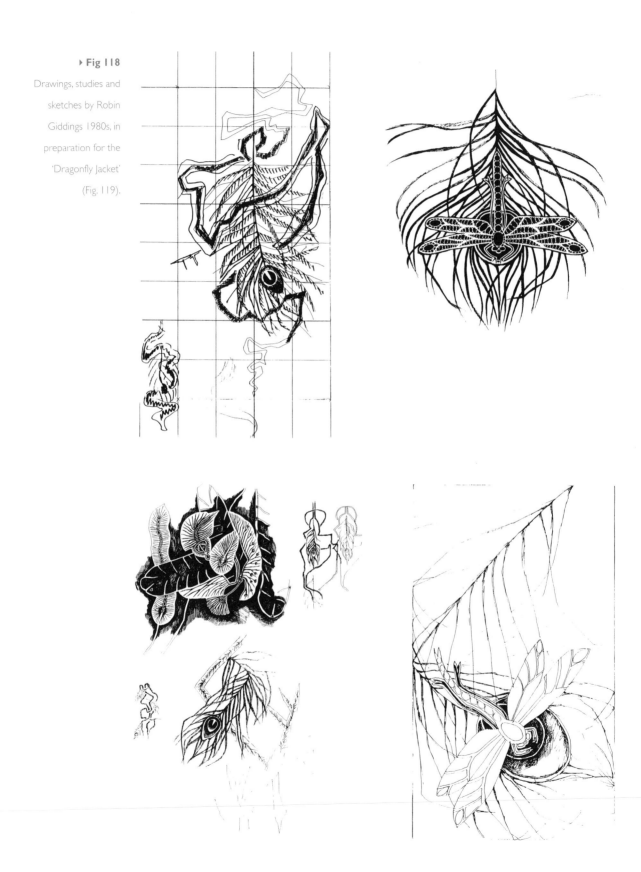

▸ **Fig 118**

Drawings, studies and sketches by Robin Giddings 1980s, in preparation for the 'Dragonfly Jacket' (Fig. 119).

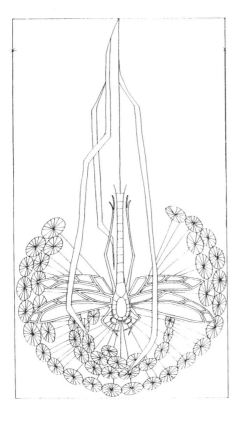

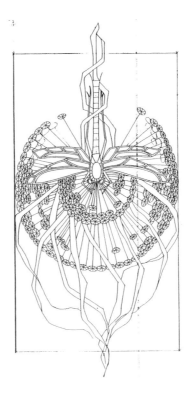

▶ Fig 119

'Dragonfly Jacket' by
Robin Giddings 1980s.
Machine-embroidered
on silk organza.

▶▶ Fig 120

'Full-length Kimono'
(detail) by Robin
Giddings 1980s.
Machine-embroidered
on 'vanished' muslin and
silk organza.

left. All these faculties contribute in one way or another to the entire process of designing. If you remember how you approached your exercises throughout this book, you will understand how this is so. Read now the following statements so that you might persuade yourself that drawing is not so terrifying but a wonderful way of developing your sensitivity and a useful part of preparing designs for embroidery. '*It is in order to really see, to see even deeper, more intensely, hence to be fully aware and alive; that I draw what the Chinese call "The Ten Thousand Things" around me. Drawing is the discipline by which I constantly rediscover the world. I have learned that what I have not drawn, I have not really seen, and that when I start drawing an ordinary thing I realise how extraordinary it is - a sheer miracle.*' (Frederick Frank).

Look now at the drawings, studies and sketches by Robin Giddings (Fig. 118) and see how his jacket (Fig. 119) could not have been designed without them. Neither would his kimonos illustrated by Figs 120 and 121 have been formed without such

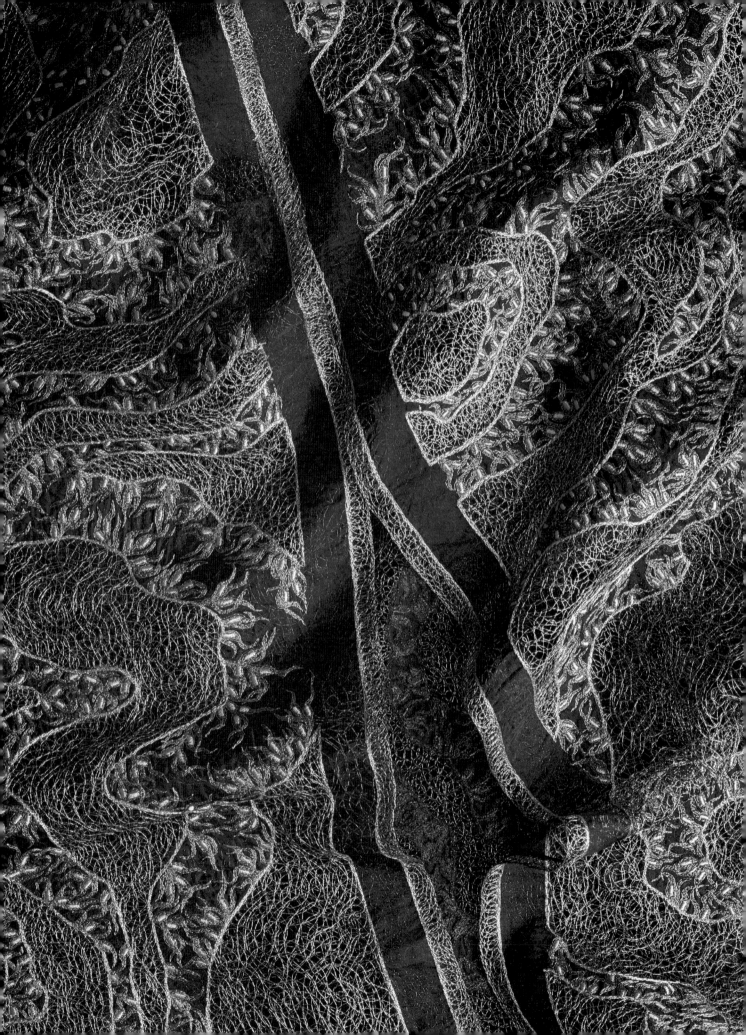

▶ **Fig 121**

'Kimono Jacket' by Robin
Giddings 1980s.
Machine-embroidered
on 'vanished' muslin and
silk organza.

preliminary investigations. Notice also how sensitive they are and interesting in their own right. I hope you are now inspired to draw!

Fluency and Flexibility

Fluency and flexibility are inextricably linked, like two sides of the same coin, which contribute to the whole of our creative potential.

Fluency refers to the extent of copiousness, speed and ease of our thinking and practice with the principles of composition. The wealthier the store we have of this information, the more likely new and fruitful ideas will emerge, provided this knowledge is used in a flexible manner.

Flexibility is the ability to adapt to new situations and adjust to new conditions. Fear of making mistakes, the employment of too rigid a rule, worrying about the end product and an overrated view of success, are all opposed to the nature of flexibility and also of fluency. You will have noticed that I have urged you to refrain from immediate judgement and censorship of your exercises throughout this book and to defer appropriate criticism until later on. As designers we need to develop habits in fluency and flexibility by producing numerous and varied possibilities without fear of judgement and rejection so that we accumulate many possibilities from which later assessment, relevant selection and appropriate evaluation can be made. Who knows? You may, by this means, make an important discovery which is irrelevant to the present task but extremely relevant to another.

'How', you may now ask, 'can I do this?' My advice so far has been to engage in some form of relaxed but attentive exercise prior to starting work. Added to this, ensure that you work for short periods. Organise your daily life so that your practice is regular even if it is only a little each day. Work at speed either quickly or slowly but avoid extremes of haste and dithering. Recognise that part of the whole design process involves a lot of preparation at the beginning. 'Genius,' said Thomas Carlyle, 'is

'Fluent ideation is demonstrated by the thinker who generates many ideas; the yardstick of fluency is quantity. Flexible ideation is exhibited by a thinker who expresses diverse ideas; the measure of flexibility is variety.'

Robert H. McKim

117

➤ **Fig 122**
Samples by Robin
Giddings 1980s and
1990s. Machine-
embroidered on
'vanished' muslin and
silk organza.

the transcendent capacity of taking trouble first of all.' In between your work periods take a rest, go for a walk or engage in another activity altogether. Even contrive to have a number of projects proceeding alongside each other like the numerous samples by Robin Giddings (Fig. 122). Be prepared for some length of uncertainty at any stage in any one of your projects. Allow this incubation period to exist. Sleep on it and let your creative thought processes work unconsciously. Avoid the temptation of giving up in despair. Nurture patience and perseverance which Cennino Cennini described as 'constancy' and you will be rewarded with a sudden flash of insight. You will be surprised how solutions seem to come from nowhere! This illumination then requires confirmation and realisation which in itself may take time, cause changes and developments before eventual completion. Finally, be content in the knowledge that you may not be completely satisfied with your achievements. As one solution leads to a further problem so also does one achievement lead to another project. The design process is not one but many. Yet the many are part of one continuum - a lifetime's adventure and a voyage of discovery.

'That virtue of originality that men so strain after is not newness, as they vainly think - there is nothing new. It is only genuineness.'

John Ruskin

Originality

Do you worry about being original? Then, try not to! You already possess originality. As Robert Henri wrote, '*You could not get rid of it even if you wanted to. It will stick to you and show you up for better or worse in spite of all you or anyone else can do.*' He continues, '*Don't bother about your originality, set yourself just as free as you can and your originality will take care of you.*'

Originality is the ability to react and respond naturally and honestly. Originality comes from within not from without, however much we are necessarily influenced and even inspired by others and our surroundings. Originality is at the very centre of all the capabilities which we are considering and is nurtured by them. Leave your originality alone and it will be fostered by the development of your sensitive awareness, fluency and flexibility. Be true and genuine to yourself and to your own unique creative process.

Now look at Figs 123 and 124 and understand how Pat McCoy's creative process is original to her. The main inspiration and resource for her work is Romanesque architecture, medieval illuminations and embroidery. The carvings on the tympana and doorways of churches and abbeys in France are of special interest. 'Isaiah' (Fig. 123) is derived from such an image on the church at Souillac.

Pat McCoy often visits these places to study such works by taking photographs and drawing in a

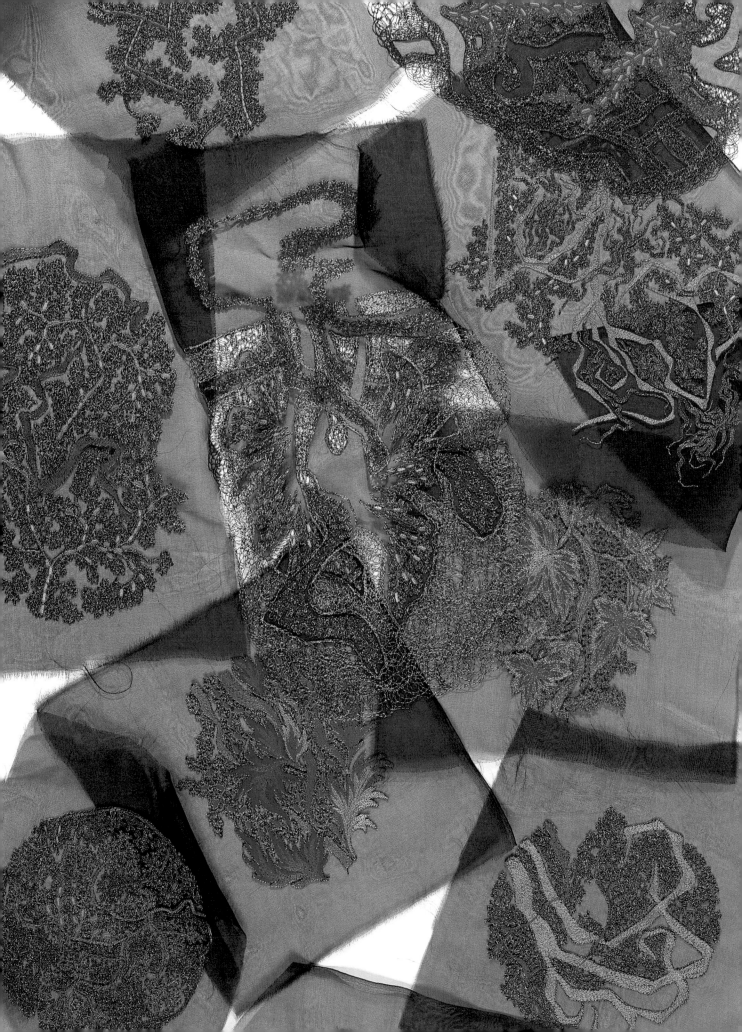

Chichester Reliefs XVI cents

Malmesbury Abbey Wiltshire

▶ **Fig 123** 'Isaiah' by Pat McCoy. Machine embroidery with painted elements. (Photograph: Pat McCoy.).

variety of media as you see in Fig. 124. This kind of research is an essential part of her design process. Read now in her own words how she embodies with line, colour and texture her expressive and symbolic intentions.

'I try to convey in my work a sense of history and the mystery that surrounds it. There is, on one hand, the clearly understood element which is well documented; on the other hand, there is the lost and blurred element which has come to us in the form of myth and legend. I am fascinated by the merging of fact and fantasy. Therefore, the rounded curves from weathered architectural carvings whose blurred images often contain contrasting clear-cut passages, which have escaped the ravages of time, are particularly suitable sources for my work. They inspire me creatively and spiritually. The disappearance and emergence of an image is central to the content of my work…

'Isaiah' represents such fragments of history which can be lost and found with startling contrasts of obscurity and clarity. Birth and decay not only of man and nature but also of ideas, kingdoms and politics also have disappearing and emerging qualities. Such concepts become a cycle. Therefore my lines and shapes are rounded to express order from chaos and the continuity of life. …

'I have used the complementary colours of yellow-oranges and purple-blues to express clarity and give vibrancy to the composition. To express obscurity I have chosen only muted and dull colours. Similarly, there are strong contrasts of tone in the central and

'Many that are first shall be last; and the last shall be first.'

St. Matthew

focal areas whereas I have blended the tonal values in outer areas so that they merge into each other in order to represent the age-worn aspect of stone carvings and evoke lost knowledge through the mists of time..

'Texture is also contrasted for similar purposes by using mixed media and different techniques. There are areas which are just painted, areas which are collaged with various textured materials and which have been partially stitched by machine very quickly and dragged back and forth creating a loose, rough surface and a feeling of deterioration, and areas where the stitching is dense, sharp and in relief. All these devices are employed to represent the contrasts between the clear and the obscure, disappearance and emergence, fact and fantasy.'

Conclusion

I often say to my students, partly in jest, *'You ought to have done this course before you come on it!'* You may remember reading in the Introduction that I asked you to treat this book as a progressive course and consider each exercise as an individual piece of a jigsaw puzzle whose picture as a whole will gradually emerge and be revealed to you at the end. Now that you have arrived here you may be thinking that the book should have been written in reverse order. Process of design determines the principles of composition which guide how we use the formal elements. In other words: the first should be last ;

◀◀ **Fig 124** Drawings, photographs and sketches. by Pat McCoy 1997 to 1998. Preliminary studies for 'Isaiah' (Fig. 129).

and the last should be first. However, I have chosen to do otherwise because when I learn something new I need to perform practical exercises that exemplify principles and processes which come to my understanding later rather than earlier. I hope you agree and approve!

The process of designing is not so sequential as it is holistic. Now that you have read the book as a whole and performed all of the exercises, you could read it all over again at a more informed level; but this time, in any order you like so that you can make cross-references, transfer your

understanding of practices, principles and processes from one to another and continue your adventures with colour and design for as long as you like.

Finally, I leave you with the words from the fifteenth-century Renaissance philosopher Pico Della Mirandola, who, writing about the gift of creativity being inherent in all human beings, imagined God speaking to Adam as representing each one of his readers. Written over 500 years ago these words are as applicable now as they were to his students then.

'Thou constrained by no limits in accordance with thine own free will shall ordain for thyself the limits of thy nature. We have set thee at the world's centre that thou mayest from thence more easily observe whatever is in the world … so that with freedom of choice and honour, as maker and moulder of thyself, thou mayest fashion thyself into whatever shape thou prefer. Thou shalt have the power to denigrate into lower forms of life … thou shalt have the power to be reborn into the higher forms which are divine.'

From The Oration on the Dignity of Man, *Pico della Mirandola*

Glossary

Words and phrases can have different meanings for different people at different times and in different places. My definitions may not meet the approval or agreement of all. However, the following brief descriptions refer to how I have intended these terms to be understood in the context of this book:

Alternation Reciprocal repetition of motifs or any of the formal elements.

Analogy A similarity, equivalent, metaphor, parable, simile, e.g., analogous colours are similar colours.

Analytical Refers to the ability to abstract particular parts or specific relations from generalities.

Assessment The ability to observe objectively, and to understand what has been done and is being done.

Asymmetrical balance The harmonious composition of elements by means of proportion, ratio or the just relationship between repetition and contrast.

Attention The ability to be fully observant without being distracted by irrelevancies.

Balance Matching, bringing into equilibrium, regulating extreme differences, equalisation.

Chromatic Value The quality that refers to any colour value within the range between bright and dull.

Colours The constituent parts of decomposed rays of light and the general name given to those elements: red, orange, yellow, green, blue, violet and purple.

Colour temperature The quality in colours which render their being warm or cool.

Complementary Refers to an element or quality which usually contrasts with, or is in opposition to, another element or quality. e.g.. red and green, dark and pale, rough and smooth.

Complexity Intricacy, complication and involvement.

Composition The harmonious relation of all parts, elements and qualities of a whole.

Concurrent The running or existing together of two or more activities to which attention is given alternately but not simultaneously.

Configuration The shape, aspect or character produced by the relative position of its parts.

Content (noun) The embodiment of intention by the form of composition.

Contrast The emphasis of differences between things, elements or qualities by close juxtaposition.

Creativity The imaginative thought processes which govern the ability to bring elements into form.

Cross-hatching A method of drawing by means of crossed parallel lines in order to achieve a type of shading or certain coloured effects.

Design The plan or organisation of all parts of an activity or any created object, to compose a coherent order and unity.

Direction Position or attitude, e.g. vertical, horizontal or oblique.

Discipline An area or field in which an artist or designer works e.g. embroidery, drawing, quilting etc.

Discord Extreme contrast, opposition or conflict.

Dominance A preponderant, predominant or principal quality or element in composition.

Drawing The representation, portrayal and realisation of a person's response to the world.

Dynamic Refers to the characteristic of movement, life and action.

Elements The components that contribute to the structure and substance of any created object such as edge, line, shape, form, tone, colour and texture.

Evaluation The ability to recognise the value in that which has been done and is being done for present and future use.

Expression The power or act of conveying individual thoughts and feelings.

Figure and ground A phrase that refers to the alternation between 'subject' or motif and its surroundings or background.

Flexibility The ability to adapt and adjust to new or different situations and conditions.

Fluency The ability to be speedy and copious in thinking and performing.

Focal point The position of direct interest.

Form (noun) A shape resulting from the composition of the elements.

Form (verb) To create, construct and make.

Formal elements see 'Elements'.

Golden Section The 'ideal' ratio discovered first by the geometrician, Euclid, and later the mathematician, Fibonacci, and known to manifest itself in many natural forms.

Gradation A sequence or transition of any formal element from one stage or extreme to another; a scale or successive steps.

Harmony The balanced combinations of various qualities and elements, usually comprising those that are both similar and complementary.

Hatching A method of shading with parallel lines.

Holistic Refers to the ability to understand whole things altogether at once.

Hue The quality that distinguishes one particular kind of colour from another such as a blue-green and a yellow-green.

Inspiration An enlightening influence.

Integrity The state of wholeness and completeness, entire in and of itself.

Intuition The power of the mind to react and respond instinctively and spontaneously.

Knowledge That which is discovered and understood (an empirical definition only).

Law An authoritative statute that governs rules but itself is governed by principles.

Line A term used in three different ways: (a) that which represents an edge or contour of a shape; (b) a very thin shape; (c) that which denotes direction.

Local colour The intrinsic colour of any particular object such as a red rose.

Local colour tone The intrinsic tonal value of any particular object such as a dark red rose or a pale red rose.

Logical Refers to the ability to reason and to reach conclusions by following an ordered sequence of thought.

Medium The materials with which the artist, designer or embroiderer works, e.g. paint, pencils, fabric and thread.

Monochrome The same hue of any colour but of different tonal and chromatic values.

Originality The genuineness, sincerity and truthfulness of thought and action.

Perception The detection and recognition of sensations and stimuli within the environment.

Point A dot, a starting position or the beginning of a line.

Principle A fundamental theory which governs laws.

Process Thinking, doing and proceeding with awareness.

Progression see Gradation.

Proportion The relationship of measurements.

Radiation The divergence from a central point.

Rational Refers to the ability to make decisions based upon information, facts and reasons.

Ratio see Proportion.

Realisation That which has been made manifest and real such as drawing, design or embroidery.

Repetition Recurrence of any of the formal elements.

Rhythm Proportioned intervals between or among the formal elements.

Rules Guidelines to assist the process and practice of any activity or exercise.

Scale see Gradation.

Sensitivity The ability to be exceptionally aware and appreciative of impressions.

Shade (noun) A dark tone.

Shade (verb) To darken, such as with pencil lines in drawing and designing.

Shape An area perceived in two dimensions.

Simplicity Reduction, plainness or immediate clarity.

Simultaneous contrast The optical illusion of perceiving the opposite or complementary qualities between juxtaposed elements.

Subordinance The positive opposite of dominance, subdued or secondary quality or element in composition.

Symbolic Refers to the quality of any of the formal elements representing another quality e.g. bright yellow signifies generosity, glory or divinity; dull yellow signifies cowardice, deceit or treachery.

Symmetry Reverse repetition on an equal number of sides of parts of a composition.

Texture The surface quality of any physical substance.

Tint A light or pale tone.

Tone (or tonal value.) The quality that distinguishes anything within the range between light and dark.

Unity Cohesion, wholeness or integrity.

Value see Tone *and also* Chromatic value.

Bibliography

Alford, Lady Marion, M., **Needlework as Art**, Samson Low 1886, republished by E. P. Publishing 1975.

Arnason, H.H., **A History of Modern Art**, revised edition, Thames and Hudson 1977.

Benham, W. Gurney, **Cassell's Classified Quotations**, Cassell 1921.

Berger René, **The Language of Art**, Thames and Hudson 1963.

Bloomer, Carolyn M., **Principles of Visual Perception**, Van Nostrand Reinhold 1976.

Cameron, Julia, **The Artist's Way**, Pan Books 1995.

Cennini, Cennino, **The Craftsman's Handbook**, Dover 1954 (Translated by Daniel V. Thompson Jr.
    from 'Il Libro dell' Arte').

Chipp, Herschel B., **Theories of Modern Art**, University of California Press 1968.

Collingwood, R.G., **The Principles of Art**, Oxford University Press 1979.

Day Lewes, F., **Art in Needlework**, B.T. Batsford Ltd. 1990.

de Sausmarez, Maurice, **Basic Design: The Dynamics of Visual Form**, Herbert Press 1992.

Edwards, Betty,. **Drawing on the Right Side of the Brain**, Souvenir Press 1981.

Ellinger, Richard G., **Colour Structure and Design**, Van Nostrand Reinhold Company 1980.

Field, Dick., **Change in Art Education**, Routledge and Kegan Paul 1970.

Frank, Frederick, **The Awakened Eye**, Wildhouse(UK), Bookwise (Australia) 1980.

Gage, John., **Colour and Culture**, Thames and Hudson 1995.

Graves, Maitland, **The Art of Colour and Design**, McGraw-Hill Book Company 1951.

Hamilton, George Heard, **Painting and Sculpture in Europe 1880-1940**, revised edition, Penguin 1978.

Henri, Robert, **The Art Spirit**, Harper and Row 1984.

Howard, Constance, **Embroidery and Colour**, B.T. Batsford Ltd. 1976

Itten Johannes, **The Elements of Colour**, Van Nostrand Reinhold 1922.

Jones, Owen, **The Grammar of Ornament**, Day and Son 1856, republished by Omega Books Ltd 1986.

Kandinsky, Wassily, **Concerning the Spiritual in Art**, Republished by Dover 1997.

Klee, Paul, **On Modern Art**, Faber and Faber 1979.

Loomis, Andrew, **The Eye of the Painter**, Pitman and Sons Ltd. 1962.

Lowenfeld, Victor, **Creative and Mental Growth**, fifth edition Macmillan 1970.

Malins, Frederick, **Understanding Paintings: The Elements of Composition**, Phaidon 1928.

McKim, Robert H., **Experiences in Visual Thinking**, second edition, Wadsworth 1980.

Morris, May, **Decorative Needlework**, Joseph Hughes and Co. 1893.

Murray, Peter and Murray, Linda, **A Dictionary of Art and Artists**, third edition, Penguin 1975.

Read, Herbert, **Education Through Art**, Faber and Faber 1958.

Ruskin, John, **The Elements of Drawing**, Dover 1971.

Saunders, Sally, **Royal School of Needlework, Embroidery Techniques**, B.T. Batsford Ltd. 1998.

Wood, James, **The Nuttall Dictionary of Quotations**, Frederick Warne 1930.

Index

Numbers in italic denote pictures